European Union Law

Nutcases – your essential revision and starter guides

- Provides you with in-depth case analysis of the facts, principles and decision of the most important cases in an area of law

- Incorporates colour to help distinguish cases and legislation and aid ease of use

- Presents the text in bite-size chunks and includes bullets where appropriate to aid navigation, assimilation and retention of information

- Breaks the subject down into key topics to enable you to easily identify and concentrate on particular topics

- Opens each chapter with a short introduction to outline the key concepts covered and condense complex and important information

- Includes boxed "think points" at the end of each ter providing further case analysis

- Fully indexed by individual cases and topics

Available from all good booksellers

NUT**SHELLS**

European Union Law

EIGHTH EDITION

by
MIKE CUTHBERT, LLM, BSc (ECON), BA (Law), FRSA
formerly Senior Tutor in Law
University of Northampton

SWEET & MAXWELL

THOMSON REUTERS

First edition – 1994
Second edition – 1997
Third edition – 2000
Fourth edition – 2003
Fifth edition – 2006
Sixth edition – 2009
Seventh edition – 2012

Published in 2015 by Thomson Reuters (Professional) UK Limited
trading as Sweet & Maxwell, Friars House, 160 Blackfriars Road, London, SE1 8EZ
(Registered in England and Wales, Company No. 1679046.
Registered Office and address for service:
Aldgate House, 33 Aldgate High Street, London EC3N 1DL)

For further information on our products and services, visit
www.sweetandmaxwell.co.uk

Typeset by YHT Ltd
Printed in Great Britain by
Ashford Colour Press, Gosport, Hants

No natural forests were destroyed to make this product;
only farmed timber was used and re-planted

A CIP catalogue record for this book is available from the British Library.

ISBN: 978-0-414-03590-4

Contents

Using this book

CHAPTER INTRODUCTIONS open every chapter, providing an overview of the topic to be discussed.

The Basis of Interv

INTRODUCTION

The process of judicial review involve
made by bodies exercising public
legality of these decisions

...are in a
...fendant is involved in a
to win.

CHECKPOINT

Approach adopted to incidents b
sporting events:
- In *Condon v Basi* (CA, 1985), a "
  local amateur football match w
- In *Watson v British Boxing Boc
  out that where the plaintiff c
  boxing ring he does not con
  safety arrangements by t'

CHECKPOINTS highlight key concepts and define complex terms, boxed for easy identification and revision.

KEY CASES present the facts and judgments in the most influential case-law, boxed for easy identification and revision.

...comp
...d secondly, since the
plaintiff cannot be said to cons
time (*Baker v T. E. Hopkins & Sor*

KEY CASE

**DANGER INVITES RESCUE; RESCUERS
RESCUE IS TO SAVE LIFE OR LIMB.**
Chadwick v British Transport Com
assisted at the scene of a train cra
as a result of what he saw was he
was in no personal danger (for '
generally see Ch.2).

LEGISLATION HIGHLIGHTERS provide
extracts of the significant legislation,
boxed for easy identification and revision.

> **LEGISLATION HIGHLIGHTER**
>
> Section 149 of the Road Traffic Act (19
> the driver's liability to his passenger
> means that the *volenti* defence is now
> road traffic accidents.

4. Rescuers
If the defendant's negligence endang
rescue attempt is reasonably fores
nes v Harwood (CA, 1935))
d is actually the d

COLOUR CODING throughout to
help distinguish cases and legislation
from the narrative.

equent case law has decided
(a) Jews are an ethnic group (*Seide v*
(b) Gypsies are an ethnic group (*CRE v*
(c) Rastafarians are not an ethnic group
     ment [1993] I.R.L.R. 284)
(d) Jehovah's Witnesses are not an ethnic
     Norwich City College case 1502237/97
(e) RRA covers the Welsh (*Gwynedd CC v*
(f) Both the Scots and the English are co
     "national origins" but not by "ethn
     Board v Power [1997], *Boyce v Brit*

should be noted that Sikh
re also

DIAGRAMS AND FLOWCHARTS condense and visually
represent detailed information.

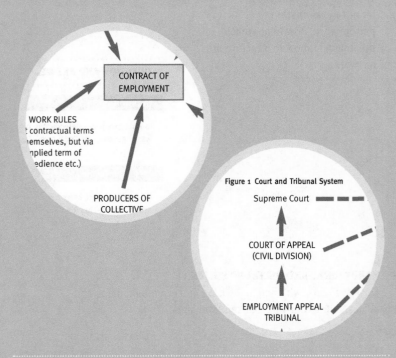

CONTRACT OF
EMPLOYMENT

WORK RULES
: contractual terms
iemselves, but via
nplied term of
edience etc.)

PRODUCERS OF
COLLECTIVE

Figure 1 Court and Tribunal System

Supreme Court

COURT OF APPEAL
(CIVIL DIVISION)

EMPLOYMENT APPEAL
TRIBUNAL

END OF CHAPTER REVISION
CHECKLISTS identify the key take-aways from the chapter.

..us held the
liable because the pre
alleged negligence that, as the
criminal offence.

REVISION CHECKLIST

You should now understand:

☐ **The conditions within which the
and the overlap between the def**

☐ *Volenti* **is a complete defence ar
because it is more flexible;**

END OF CHAPTER QUESTION AND ANSWER SECTION is a chance to practice what you have learnt, with advice on relating knowledge to examination performance, how to approach the question, how to structure the answer.

....
QUESTION AND ANSWE
....

QUESTION

To what extent is a defendant in a t was engaged in an illegal activity a

APPROACH TO THE ANSWER

Outline the effect of *ex tu* action can be founde

HANDY HINTS AND USEFUL WEBSITES

close the book, with helpful revision and examination tips and advice, along with a list of useful websites.

HANDY HINTS

Examination questions in employme. either essay questions or problem ques format and in what is required of the ex of question in turn.

Students usually prefer one type normally opting for the problem ques examinations are usually set in a wa least one of each style of question

Very few, if any, questions
ows about a topic, and it make a p

USEFUL WEBSITES

Official Information
www.parliament.uk—very user-friendly.
www.direct.gov.uk—portal for governme
www.opsi.gov.uk—Office of Public Secto
and statutory instruments available
www.dca.gov.uk—Department for Con
www.dca.gov.uk/peoples-rights/hum
Unit at the Department for Con
www.homeoffice.gov.uk/police/
the **Police and Criminal**

Table of Cases

Table of United Kingdom Legislation

Table of European Legislation

Regulations

Directives

Introduction

The study of European law does cause anxiety for some students because it seems to be so different from the common law approach that they are familiar with from their other studies of English law. However, as a member of the European Union the United Kingdom is bound to follow EU law and its courts must provide a remedy for those who seek to enforce it or claim rights under it.

An understanding of European law is considered so important that the professional legal bodies representing solicitors and barristers in the UK have made it a compulsory subject for all those students who wish to qualify as a legal professional. This is in recognition that not only businesses but also individuals are affected by European law in their everyday lives as employees, citizens or consumers.

To support your understanding of European law this book attempts to provide an overview of the key definitions, cases and principles that have been developed since the 1950s. The chapters contain a short introduction plus a list of the key points that you should familiarise yourself with. Key points and cases are boxed to show the importance they have for the topic.

All this is preparation for you to understand European law better and to help you prepare for examinations or assessments. Each chapter has a question that can be used to test yourself with a list of main points that you should include in your answer.

The most recent EU Treaty is the Treaty of Lisbon and this is explained and analysed in the appropriate chapters of this book. The outcome of the Treaty of Lisbon is two separate documents—the Treaty on European Union (TEU) and the Treaty on the Functioning of the EU (TFEU). This is to some extent a compromise because of the failure to ratify a constitutional treaty in 2008 and it means that there is not the single document that was envisaged when the reform process started in 2001.

The European Union Institutions

....
BACKGROUND

When the TEU came into force on November 1, 1993 it became legally correct to refer to the European Community (EC). The word "economic" was dropped to reflect the fact that there had been a change of emphasis towards non-economic provisions such as citizenship. It also became usual to refer to the European Union at the expense of the European Community. This was confirmed by the Treaty of Lisbon. There were originally three Communities, with the European Coal & Steel Community (ECSC) being established in 1952 and the EC together with EURATOM coming in 1957. However, the ECSC had a fixed life of 50 years so it ceased to exist in 2002. The policy areas of coal and steel were subsumed into the EC Treaty. Thus we now have two Communities, but the European Community is the most important pillar of the EU and the EC Treaty, as amended by the TEU and TFEU, still dominates. This will be observed in this book, as you will see repeated reference to the EC Treaty as the Union has developed. (Chapter 12 looks at the TEU and its subsequent amendment by the Treaty of Amsterdam, the Treaty of Nice and more importantly the Treaty of Lisbon in more detail see p.174.)

In 1952 the first of the European Communities was established in the form of the European Coal and Steel Community (ECSC). Although this had followed on from other bodies established by an international agreement, such as the Council of Europe (1949), the development of this Community was characterised by a clear transfer of rights to special institutions. These rights had been previously seen as sovereign to national governments. In 1957 the European Economic Community (now simply the European Union under the TEU) and EURATOM were established. Initially the three European Communities had different institutions and in the case of the Commission a different name in the sense that for the purposes of the ECSC it was called the High Authority. The Merger Treaty of 1965 that made the institutions common to all three Communities changed all this. The Three Pillars of the TEU were replaced by the Treaty of Lisbon in 2009 to reflect the failure of the implementation of the Convention on the Future of the European Union proposals in the Constitutional Treaty. This is discussed in more detail in

Ch.12. Although we now have a European Union it is still common to refer to the European Community as it is built upon the dominance of the European Community Treaty but legally now you should refer to the European Union.

....

EUROPEAN PARLIAMENT

It is Title III of the Lisbon Treaty which lays out the "Institutional Provisions". The first institution dealt with is the European Parliament (EP), although it was initially referred to as the European Assembly in the 1957 EC Treaty. Perhaps, given the democratic underpinning that is now explicitly stated in art.10 TEU, we now assume this to be essential for the EU, but the original Parliament was not democratically elected nor did it fulfil any of the functions we might identify as the characteristics of a parliament, of any tradition. The membership was originally nominated by the governments of the Member States (MS) to exercise advisory and supervisory powers. However, its place as the first institution laid out in the Treaty may have more significance for the "vision" of Europe shared by the authors of the Treaty in the political context of the 1950's. The current discussions between those who see the Union as having a purely economic function as against those with a wider political "federal" viewpoint have their philosophical base in the Treaty. The original Parliament was very weak because the establishment and success of the EC depended upon a strong role for the governments of the MS and thus the Council of Ministers (now called 'the Council' in the Lisbon Treaty). However, having recognised the need for a "democratic" institution in the Treaty it was possible to strengthen its powers and thus its role over time. This is what happened and is happening with regard to the European Parliament.

The Lisbon Treaty did not come into effect until after the 2009 elections to the EP so those elections took place on the old allocation of EP seats. Article 14(2) TEU states that there shall be a maximum of 750 MEPs plus the President of the EP with a minimum threshold of 6 and a maximum of 96 seats for any MS. This allocation is based on the relative size of population for each MS and is shown in Table 2.1 below. When the Treaty of Lisbon did come into force an Inter-Governmental Conference was held on June 23, 2010 to allow the additional MEPs to take up their seats with all the MEPs coming up for election in 2014. The allocation of MEPs to MS no longer appears in the Treaties as art.14(2) TEU allows the Council by unanimity, on the initiative and consent of the EP, to decide on the composition of the EP. Direct elections specified under art.14(3) TEU have taken place every five years since 1979.

Table 2.1 Number of Representatives by Member State 2014

Member State	No of MEPs
France	74
Germany	96
Italy	73
United Kingdom	73
Poland	51
Spain	54
Romania	32
Austria	18
Belgium	21
Bulgaria	17
Czech Republic	21
Greece	21
Hungary	21
Netherlands	26
Portugal	21
Sweden	20
Croatia	11
Denmark	13
Finland	13
Ireland	11
Slovakia	13
Lithuania	11
Estonia	6
Latvia	8
Slovenia	8
Cyprus	6
Luxembourg	6
Malta	6

Source: European Council Decision (2013/312/EU)

The original delegates, nominated by Member States, have been replaced by directly elected Members of the European Parliament (MEPs) who represent their constituents. All elections to the European Parliament are based on the principle of proportional representation, unlike under the normal British principle of "first past the post". This led to the novel introduction on the British mainland of the results of the 1999 European Parliamentary elections being based on a "list" system rather than the traditional "one MEP—one constituency" of previous elections in Britain. Since the introduction of direct elections in 1979 the character of the European Parliament has changed. This is reflected not only in the procedures that the MEPs have adopted for themselves where they have become more professional, but also in the demands they have made to increase their role and powers within the Union. MEPs basically want to have the role of a "parliament". Although this concept varies between the Member States, the common characteristic is the role in the legislative process and the accountability of the "government" to the MEPs. There is no "government" in the national sense within the EU, thus the emphasis has been on the involvement in the legislative process and the approval of the EU budget. The Single European Act (SEA) recognised this and introduced the cooperation procedure as one of the legislative procedures. The TEU took this a step further with the co-decision procedure and the subsequent Treaty of Amsterdam and Treaty of Nice have consolidated this development. The failed Constitutional Treaty 2004, discussed in Ch.12, was intended to take this further but this has now been achieved by the Treaty of Lisbon. Article 14(1) TEU states that the EP shall exercise jointly with the Council the legislative and budgetary functions of the EU.

The 2014 EP elections resulted in the European People's Party (EPP) being the largest group within the parliament with 221 MEPs. The outcome was as follows:

Table 2.2 Political Groups and % of Votes

Political Group	% of vote	No. of MEPS
European People's Party (EPP)	29.4	221
Alliance of Socialist & Democrats (S&D)	25.4	191
Conservatives & Reformists (ECR)	9.3	70
Alliance of Liberals & Democrats (ALDE)	8.9	67
European United Left/Nordic Green Left (GUE/NGL)	6.9	52
The Greens/European Free Alliance (Greens/EFA)	6.7	50
Freedom & Direct Democracy Group (EFDD)	4.3	48
Non-attached Members (NI)	7.1	52
	Total	751

More detailed information is available on the EP website: *http://www.europarl.europa.eu*

DECISION-MAKING PROCEDURES

The role of the European Parliament has increased with the Treaty of Lisbon and it now participates as an equal with the Council in the legislative and budgetary process associated with art.288 TFEU. Article 225 TFEU gives the EP the authority to request the Commission to submit any appropriate proposal on matters that it considers that the Union should act. Previously this was something only the Council could do (see art.241 TFEU). Requests have to be made to the European Commission because under the Treaty they are given the role of initiator and producer of draft proposals.

As a result of increasing the powers of the European Parliament the Union's decision-making procedures became very complex, but the Treaty of Lisbon has simplified this dramatically by concentrating on what was called the Co-decision, but is now referred to as the "ordinary legislative procedure" (art.289 TFEU). There are other decision-making procedures, which vary with the area of legislation under consideration.

Consultation: This is the original procedure with a single Parliamentary reading that was laid down by the EC Treaty in 1957. The voting in the Council of Ministers has to be unanimous. See Case 138/79 *Roquette v Council* below. This procedure is rarely used now.

The Ordinary Legislative Procedure (previously the Co-decision): (Article 294 TFEU) This is the most important procedure with regard to legislation. The Co-decision procedure was introduced by the TEU in 1993 and extensively developed by the Treaty of Amsterdam and the Treaty of Nice. Under this procedure the Parliament is given the power to prevent legislation being adopted. Generally qualified majority voting (qmv) is required in the Council except on two issues where unanimity applies. (See Ch.3 below, p.30). Examples of policy areas under the co-decision procedures included: transport policy; development aid; Trans-European Networks; employment policy; public health; and equal opportunities. Under art.288 TFEU the EU institutions can legislate on any matter within the Union's competences (see diagram on p.34).

Consent: The SEA originally introduced an 'assent' procedure but this is now referred to as the 'consent' procedure. Its scope has been increased by the TEU and it now applies in the case of international agreements, Treaty decisions and accession of new members. It means that the European Parliament must agree for the proposal to be implemented. An example is art.49 TEU which states that the EP must consent to any new MS.

Budget: This is covered by a procedure in arts 313–319 TFEU, which gives

HOW IS EU LAW MADE?
Who are the players and what are their roles?

Role of European Commission as
INITIATOR

COR	European Parliament	ESC
	First Reading	

COUNCIL OF MINISTERS

Council Approves	Council Does Not Approve Adopts Common Position

European Parliament
Second Reading

European Parliament
Proposes Amendments

Conciliation Committee
IF NO AGREEMENT THE MEASURE FALLS

equal authority to the European Parliament in relation to budgetary matters. See the EP and the Union's Annual Budget below, p.9.

However, whatever weight is given to the views of the European Parliament, the right to be consulted must be respected. Failure to follow this procedural requirement may lead to the measure being declared invalid. This happened in the cases of Case 138/79 *Roquette v Council* and Case 139/79 *Maizena v Council*, both reported in 1980.

The European Parliament has certain characteristics similar to national parliaments. There are a number of standing committees that mirror the major policy areas of the Community. These committees carry out investigations and hear evidence from experts and interested parties, including the Commission. They also issue reports. In addition parliamentary questions are an important element of control over the Commission. Under art.230 TFEU the Commission must reply orally or in writing to questions put to it by MEPs. In fact the Council and foreign ministers also take part in this process. It is common practice now for the President of the Council of Ministers to make a statement at the commencement of their Presidency outlining their objectives and to report to the Parliament at the end of their term on the outcomes.

KEY CASE

CASE 138/79 ROQUETTE V COUNCIL AND CASE 139/79 MAIZENA V COUNCIL

The Council had sent a proposal to the EP for a measure it wished to enter into force on July 1, 1979. There was a delay in the EP due to the opinion of the Parliamentary Agriculture Committee being rejected in the plenary session. The EP offered to have a special meeting to approve the measure but the Council ignored this and adopted the measure on June 25, 1979.

Held: In its judgment the CJEU stated that the requirement of consultation implies that the Parliament has expressed its opinion. This had not happened so the Court declared the measure void.

Commentary: This case illustrates the role that the CJEU plays under the Treaties with regard to judicial review. The Treaties are the 'constitution' of the EU and all the institutions have to act according to the powers and procedures that are provided there. There had been a 'failure of an essential procedural requirement' in this instance.

European Ombudsman

As with national parliaments, those who are affected by particular policies or proposals can complain to their representative. The TEU allows for such petitions to be made to their MEP but in addition there is the provision in art.228 TFEU for the appointment by the EP of an Ombudsman to deal with complaints from any citizen of the Union, including those undertakings with a registered office in a Member State. The complaints can deal with any instances of maladministration. This encompasses the activities of all Union institutions and bodies, excluding the CJEU and the General Court when acting in their judicial role.

European Parliament and the Commission

The original treaties of the then EC made the European Commission responsible to the European Parliament but this relationship has now been developed as the EP has to approve the appointment of first the President of the Commission and the other Commissioners (art.17(7) TEU). Once appointed by the Member States and the EP the 28 Commissioners can only be removed by the EP passing a censure motion by a two-thirds majority vote and an absolute majority of its members under art.234 TFEU. Such a motion successfully passed would force the resignation of the whole Commission. Although threatened on occasion this has never happened, however, in order to avoid the motion of censure the Commission can resign, as it did on March 16, 1999 when the Commission headed by President Santer resigned at a time of accusations of fraud against particular Commissioners (See "Commissioners" below, p.14). Edith Cresson, one of the Commissioners accused, was found by the European Court of Justice in July 2006 to have been in breach of her obligations when holding that office by appointing her dental surgeon to positions that he was not qualified or experienced to hold (*Commission v Cresson* Case C-432/04).

European Parliament and the Union Budget

The right of the European Parliament to make changes to the budget in the past depended on the distinction between expenditure which is "compulsory" and other expenditure which is "non-compulsory". Compulsory expenditure covered that expenditure which is committed under Treaty provisions or Union legislation, e.g. the Common Agricultural Policy. Parliament could only propose modifications to this category of expenditure, thus giving the Council the final say in such matters. However, non-compulsory expenditure which included all expenditure which is not the inevitable consequences of Union legislation, could be amended by the majority of MEPs voting in favour of such proposals. This expenditure includes the Union's social policy, regional and industrial policies, and accounts for about 43 per cent of the total budget. For this type of expenditure it was the European Parliament that had the final control. Therefore, although the Parliament did have some powers of approval as far as the budget was concerned, these were weak with regard to compulsory expenditure, which is the vast majority of the total budget.

In 1975 the European Parliament was given increased powers in relation to the Union's budget by a conciliation procedure. The aim of these powers was to give the Parliament more effective participation in the budgetary process, by seeking agreement between the Parliament and the Council. If the Parliament refused to pass the budget as presented to it by the Council, a number of important consequences followed. First, the budget could not be implemented, which had implications for the expenditure level of the Union which is limited to one-twelfth of the previous year's budget per month (see art.315 TFEU). Second, a "conciliation committee", consisting of the Council and representatives of the European Parliament was established to try to resolve the disagreement. The European Commission assisted the work of this committee.

Ultimately the Parliament could reject the budget outright by a two-thirds vote cast by a majority of its members. Although it may reject it, the Parliament could not increase the total amount of the budget beyond the maximum rate of increase set by the Commission, unless the alteration was agreed by the Council. In 1988, in an attempt to improve the budgetary procedure, an Institutional Agreement was entered into by the Council, Commission and the European Parliament. While recognising the varying competencies of the institutions in the budgetary field, it fixed new rules for co-operation between the institutions. The Treaty of Lisbon treats the budget like any other piece of legislation so the difference in types of expenditure has been removed. The current procedure is in art.314 TFEU with the Commission submitting a draft budget to both the EP and the Council. The Council then adopts its position and this is forwarded to the EP, which can either approve it or propose amendments. If the Council does not approve the EP's amendments then a Conciliation Committee is convened with equal membership from both institutions. As can be seen this is the same as the "ordinary legislative procedure" so the Commission can take initiatives in order to reconcile the two views. If there is no agreement then the budget is not adopted and the restrictions on expenditure under art.315 TFEU would apply. This review of the budgetary powers of the EP illustrates the increased authority that has been given to the EP by successive treaties.

The Council (previously the Council of Ministers)

Article 13 TEU refers to the Council but previously this institution was referred to as the Council of Ministers which is a more accurate description. It is specifically covered in art.16 TEU and arts 204–243 TFEU. Its membership is made up of one representative of each of the 28 Member States. Although the main representative is the foreign minister of each Member State, the actual minister varies with the main business of the meeting. Thus if the Common Agricultural Policy is being discussed it will be the agricultural ministers who will attend and so on. In all there are ten different Council configurations. The presidency of the Council used to be held in rotation by each Member State for a period of six months although attempts have been made to introduce "Team Presidencies". The Treaty of Lisbon introduced greater authority to the position of the High Representative for Foreign Affairs and Security Policy (see below) and this person chairs the foreign ministers when they meet as the Foreign Affairs Council, but with this exception the representative of the Member State holding the Presidency will always chair the meetings during this period. This has been criticised on the grounds that the period is too short for individual ministers to acquire expertise in the role. There has been an attempt to resolve some of these problems by having greater coordination between the past, current and future Presidencies. This is often referred to as the "trios or troika format", introduced by the Lisbon Treaty. The three Member States work together to set long-term goals and prepare a common agenda on topics and major issues that will be addressed by the Council over an 18 month period. Each country then prepares its more detailed programme for when it is 'in the chair'.

Voting Procedures   However, the main discussion and action involving the Council has centred on its voting procedures. There are two voting procedures for the Council; unanimous and qualified majority voting (qmv). Some areas of policy specified in the Treaties require unanimity and these include taxation and asylum and immigration. Where unanimity is required it does provide a "veto" on the part of any MS (see below) but it was felt that this slowed down the development of the Union and so the Treaty of Nice reduced quite drastically the number of such policy areas. In the first EC Treaty it was envisaged that the Council would move, after the transitional period, to majority voting except for those specific matters identified by the Treaty as requiring unanimity. This was not to be a simple majority but a qualified one (qmv) on the basis of art.238 TFEU. Protocol 36 TFEU on Transitional Provisions provided the details of the allocation of votes to each Member State depending roughly upon the size of its population but with a minimum of three votes for the smallest country, Malta. These were amended when Croatia joined the EU in 2013. The "big four" of France, Germany, Italy and the UK have 29 votes. On any issue before the Council it requires a combination of the larger and smaller Member States to accumulate the necessary votes to adopt the measure. This seeks to ensure that no interest group in the Council can dominate the voting and encourages a compromise in the sense that the measure must be acceptable to a range of Member States; both large and small. The necessary voting majority is 260 or 73.9 per cent in favour of the measure. In preparation for enlargement in 2004 the Treaty of Nice introduced the possibility of a member of the Council requesting that such a majority vote also constitutes a certain per cent of the total population of the EU. This is retained in art.3(3) of the protocol and if the figure of 65 per cent is not met the act in question will not be adopted. (See Ch.12—"The TEU and Beyond", p.166.)

"Veto" The intention of the EC Treaty was hindered by the events of 1966 that led to the Luxembourg Accord or Compromise, which was instituted to obtain the co-operation of the French government in the working of the EU. This recognition of a "veto" in the sense that unanimity was required on particular issues not specified as requiring them under the Treaty, slowed down the actions of the Council in that it could not proceed faster than its slowest participating government. The governments of Denmark, Ireland, the UK, Greece, Portugal and Spain who joined in the 1970s and 1980s assumed that they did so with a power of veto on issues they considered important to them. Although they were politically shocked on occasions when they were thwarted in their attempts to exercise it, it was not until the SEA that attempts were made to speed up the decision-making process of the Council. For example, art.100(a) (now repealed) provided the legal base for adopting the measures necessary for the establishment and functioning of the internal market, and was passed to meet the target date of January 1, 1993 for completing this objective. Although academic debate still continues on whether the veto still exists, it is important to recognise the political nature of the Council. If the President of the Council is aware of the political implications of calling for a vote where a minority of the Council have strong objections, it is likely that such a vote will be postponed for further discussion.

The Simplified Revision Procedure and The European Union Act 2011

There is a mechanism under the "Simplified revision procedure" of art.48(6) TEU which allows for changes to the Treaties which in effect amount to a transfer of powers or competences from the MS without the need for a formal treaty amendment procedure. Any MS, the EP or the Commission may submit to the European Council such proposals as long as they do not increase the competences conferred on the Union by the Treaties. However, they do affect how decisions are made and this raised concerns with the UK government. Specifically, the UK government thought that this simplified revision procedure could be used to permit qualified majority voting in place of unanimity. The TEU and TFEU are large documents and there are within them certain articles which are referred to a "passerelles" or "rachet clauses". These can be used to transfer competences from the MS to the EU and thus be subject to qmv. The 2011 European Union Act provides the possibility of a positive referendum vote having to take place in the UK before the UK can agree to such action.

Democratic Control

As the European Parliament, as indicated above, has gained more authority in the legislative process it has been at the reduction of that held by the Council in the sense that they now have joint authority in the passage of legislation. Some politicians see the control of national parliaments over their government ministers as being the democratic control element of the Union. Such politicians see the European Parliament as a weak alternative and do not welcome changes to the relationship with the Council which they feel weakens the status of the Member State governments. In the UK the analogy is of the Westminster Parliament becoming like a county or local council in relation to the European Parliament. The Constitutional Treaty 2004 would have given more authority to national parliaments than they have at present but that Treaty was ratified. However, art.12 TEU and Protocol 1 to the TFEU do give a greater role to national parliaments in a number of ways. The communications between national parliaments and EU institutions is to be improved with draft Union legislative acts to be sent to them in good time for them to submit their opinions. This also has links with the principle of subsidiary (Protocol 2) which emphasises that some decisions may be more appropriate at national rather than EU level.

However, given the important role of the Council is it realistic to expect the national government ministers to play a significant role in developing EU policy as against making decisions to adopt such policies or legislation? If you look at any British minister who may be involved in a meeting of the Council, he is in charge of a government department and takes part in debates and answers questions in the House of Commons or in exceptional cases the House of Lords. As an MP there are constituent problems and interests to deal with. How much time is there for EU matters? Obviously there has to be some time because it is part of the minister's job, but a great deal of the work of the Council is undertaken by the Committee of Permanent Representatives or COREPER.

Committee of Permanent Representatives (COREPER)

Article 240 TFEU identifies the key role of this group of diplomats who represent the views or interests of their particular government. They liaise with the various government ministries and bring these views to the discussions which take place in Brussels. The idea is that when the Council meets much of the preliminary discussion has taken place and the Ministers can concentrate on those issues which may require a political compromise or are politically sensitive. Thus the Council's agenda will have "A" items, which have already been agreed in principle and "B" items where further discussion by the ministers is necessary to get agreement.

European Commission

The European Commissioners are sometimes described as a kind of European 'civil servant'. However, this is too simplistic as civil servants are merely expected to carry out the wishes of their political masters. Although the European Commission acts as the executive of the EU by implementing the policies decided by the Council and the European Parliament, they must make proposals as to what those policies should be. Such proposals made by the Commission are not always welcomed by the Council in the sense that they take a European stance against the perceived interests of the individual Member States. Much of the impetus for the legislation for the completion of the internal market came from the Commission as well as the move towards a "federal Europe". There are also examples where the authority of the EU has been extended to the embarrassment of some Member States, e.g. the directives dealing with beaches or water purity.

Commissioners There are 28 Commissioners in total, with one being nominated by each Member State. It is usual for Commissioners to have held high political office in their national governments, although once appointed they are required to act independently in the best interests of the EU and not for any individual country (art.17(3) TEU). From January 7, 1995 the term of office was extended to five years, to synchronise with the term of the European Parliament. Commissioners can be re-appointed. The Maastricht Treaty required that Parliament had to approve the appointment of the Commission and be consulted by the Member States before the President was nominated. This was strengthened by the Treaty of Amsterdam, which required the EP to approve the appointment of the President of the Commission. The President-elect of the Commission was then consulted by the Member States before they nominated the remaining Commissioners. Although the Commission acts as a collegiate body, each Commissioner is allocated a portfolio from the directorate-generals covering all Union policies. The problems in the Santer Commission in 1999 led to the strengthening of importance of the position of the President of the Commission so that he could reshuffle the allocation of the responsibilities of the Commissioners and with the approval of the rest of the Commission he could ask for an individual Commissioner to resign. The current position has consolidated this relationship in art.17 TEU whereby the European Council, after taking into account the elections to the EP, propose to the EP a candidate for the position of President of the Commission. This person has to be approved by the EP otherwise the European Council must nominate another candidate. The person appointed to be President of the Commission then plays a role in the selection of the other Commissions put forward by the MS. These Commissioners must also be approved by the EP before they can be appointed by the European Council acting by qualified voting. The President allocates the portfolios of the Commissioners and a member of the Commission shall resign if the President so requests.

The President of the Commission—2014 The outcome of the 2014 EP elections, mentioned above, showed how this procedure in art 17 TEU was interpreted by the EP. The leaders of the 2009–2014 EP decided that there should be a strict interpretation of art 17 TEU 'taking into account the elections to the EP'. They nominated candidates to be the 'Commission President' in waiting. This 'grand coalition' between the centre-right EPP, the centre-left S & D and the liberal ALDE parties gave rise to the 'Spitzenkandidaten' system. Each party thus fought the EP elections with a 'nominated President' and election debates were held in a number of Member States in the expectation that the most successful party's nominee would be put forward by the European Council to the EP for conferment. The EPP obtained the largest percentage of the votes and the largest number of MEPs and so the European Council put their candidate, Jean-Claude Juncker, forward to the EP. He was 'elected' by the EP and became President of the Commission in November 2014.

Duties of the Commission Article 17 TEU and arts 244–250 TFEU deal with the European Commission. It is art.17 TEU that shows the wide range of duties imposed on the Commission. The Commission initiate policies by making proposals, but they also act as the executive arm of the Union once a proposal has been adopted by an administrative act under art.288 TFEU. They are the "guardians of the Treaty". This covers not only questions concerning the relationship between the institutions, but more specifically the Enforcement Action under art.258 TFEU and Competition Policy of the EC. Both of these topics are dealt with in Ch.8, p.110. The Commission is responsible to the EP and art.234 TFEU facilitates the EP passing a motion of censure to remove the whole Commission as a body, as mentioned above. There is also the possibility of the European Court of Justice under art.247 TFEU compulsorily retiring a Commissioner who can no longer perform their duties or is guilty of serious misconduct.

High Representative of the Union for Foreign Affairs and Security Policy
This new post was created by the Treaty of Lisbon when it came into force on December 1, 2009. The Treaty of Amsterdam had introduced such a post,

held by Javier Solana in 1999, but the role has been widened and given more prestige. The first incumbent was Baroness Catherine Ashton who was appointed for a five year period. In addition to chairing the Foreign Affairs Council, she developed the European External Action Service (EEAS) to provide a coordinated and consistent policy reflecting the Union's external action. In 2014 Federica Mogherini was appointed to this post.

European Council

In 1974 the Heads of Government from the Member States began to meet to deal with some of the problems of political deadlock in the Council. It was not formally recognised as an institution of the EU until art.2 of the SEA stated that it should meet at least twice a year although this is now generally four times. Article 15 TEU states that "the European Council shall provide the Union with the necessary impetus for its development and shall define the general political guidelines thereof". Thus, although it has no role in the formal legislative process of the Community, the European Council does play a very important part in deciding the future political direction of the Union. The TEU in the Treaty of Lisbon also introduced the formal role of the President of the European Council. Before this change the political head of the MS which held the Presidency of the Council would take on this role but this was sometimes difficult to combine with the busy role of the prime minister or president of a MS and it also failed to provide for continuity. The appointment of a full time President of the European Council is intended to overcome these problems and to provide more focus for the role of the MS within the EU. Article 15 TEU provides for the European Council to elect by qmv a person to have this role for two and a half years, renewable once. They cannot hold any national office and chair meetings of the European Council and drive forward its work. The ex-Prime Minister of Belgium, Herman Van Rompuy was unanimously appointed to this new office when the Treaty of Lisbon came into force on December 1, 2009. He has now been succeeded in 2014 by Polish Prime Minister Donald Tusk.

Court of Justice of the European Union (CJEU)

The CJEU is the final main institution of the EU and fulfils the judicial role necessary to ensure that Union law is observed. In fact art.19 TEU is very short and states:

> "The Court of Justice of the EU shall include the Court of Justice, the General Court and specialised courts. It shall ensure that in the interpretation and application of the Treaties the law is observed. Member States shall provide remedies sufficient to ensure effective legal protection in the fields of Union law".

This is achieved via specific direct and indirect actions, which are discussed in the chapters dealing with Preliminary References and Judicial Review (Ch.6, p.175). However, the important points to note at this stage are the membership and procedures of the Court of Justice of the EU (CJEU) and the General Court. The main influences in the early formative years of the Court were the German but more predominantly the French legal tradition. This is shown in the fact that the working language of the Court is French, but more importantly in the office of Advocates-Generals.

Judges There are 28 judges in the CJEU with each Member State providing one judge. Appointed for a term of six years, the judges elect their own President of the Court who serves in that post for three years. Like all posts within the Court it is possible for the period in office to be renewed. Although this fixed but renewable term of office is not found in English courts, the attributes the judges should have are the same. Article 253 TFEU specifies, "they should be independent and qualified for the highest judicial office within their respective countries". However, an important difference is that whereas English judges are selected from barristers, and to lesser extent solicitors, judges in some Member States are chosen from a much wider field, including academic lawyers. Thus when the judges in the CJEU deliberate they are bringing together a variety of legal backgrounds which would not be found in an English court.

Advocates-Generals The post of Advocate-General is derived from the French legal system and is unknown in English law. There are nine Advocates-General appointed to the Court. They have the same backgrounds as judges, the same term of office and perhaps most importantly the same status. Therefore Advocates-Generals should not be seen as inferior to judges, as the seniority within the Court for both depends upon the date of appointment and not the designated office. Advocates-Generals are given a specific role under art.252 TFEU which states that "it should be the duty of the Advocate-General, acting with complete impartiality and independence, to make, in open court, reasoned submissions on cases brought before the Court of Justice, in order to assist the Court in the performance of" its tasks.

Judgments Unlike in senior English courts where a full judgment is given, including dissenting views, only one judgment is ever given by the CJEU. All the judges must agree to the one judgment, which is why they can appear so terse and lacking in any real discussion of the Law. They do not contain the obiter dicta as well as the ratio decidendi found in the common law tradition. Hence the importance of the Advocate-General is that she hears and reads all the evidence as a judge would do but she gives her opinion to the court as to what the judgment should be before the judges themselves reach their decision. In her opinion the Advocate-General can range over the case law of the court or if appropriate the jurisprudence of the Member States. In this way some insight is given as to the direction European Union Law may take in the future.

Workload The workload of the CJEU has increased tremendously since the Court was established in 1957. To help the court deal with cases, the judges sit in Chambers with three or five judges, but always with an odd number so that there can be a clear decision in the case. If the case before the Court concerns a Member State or the EU institutions the Grand Chamber of 13 judges may sit in judgment. In 1989 the General Court (formerly the Court of First Instance (CFI)) was set up to assist the CJEU by taking a specific jurisdiction with the safeguard of appeal to the CJEU itself. The CJEU has a general jurisdiction with regard to Union Law only fettered by the types of action specified in the Treaty. There are a number of direct actions available that include judicial review (art.263 TFEU) and actions against a Member State for failure to fulfil an obligation (arts 258 and 259 TFEU). In addition there is the special procedure for preliminary references under art.267 TFEU.

Procedures Whenever a case is brought to the CJEU, whether as a direct action which is heard in its entirety only by the Court or a request for a preliminary reference from a Member State under art.267 TFEU, it is processed by the Court Registry to ensure that the progress of the case can be recorded. This is especially important with preliminary references where the "file" of written documentation sent by the national court dominates the whole procedure. The procedure is that on receipt by the Registrar, the President of the Court will assign the case to one of the Chambers and nominate one of the judges to act as "rapporteur". The First Advocate-General will at the same time designate the Advocate-General for the case. The role of the judge rapporteur is that although all the papers will go to every judge hearing the case, only he will have studied them closely in order to produce a preliminary report. This report, together with any views expressed by the Advocate-General, will help the court decide what the relevant issues are. It may be decided that the Grand Chamber should hear the case, as normally happens with cases between the Member States or Union institutions. These early stages covering the written proceedings and the preparatory inquiry are held in private. Where oral proceedings follow, as with direct actions, these are held in open court in Luxembourg. The next stage is for the Advocate-General to deliver his opinion to the court and sometime after this the court will deliver its judgment. In order to speed up the procedure for preliminary references the CJEU may decide not to require the Advocate-General to deliver an opinion where no new point of law is concerned. In recent years some 52 per cent of the judgments of the CJEU were delivered without an opinion being given.

The future The President of the CJEU presented to the Justice Ministers of the Member States a number of proposals and ideas on the future of the judicial system of the EU in 2004. Principally he thought that the judicial system would be affected by an increase in the volume of cases due to the Economic Monetary Union (EMU), the full implementation of the Treaty of Amsterdam and the enlargement of the EU in 2004. There was also the Due Report in 2001 which looked at the future of the EU court structure. The increase to 28 Member States, the widening policy areas where the EU has competence, the potential for cases arising from aspects of criminal and family law and the implementation of the Treaty of Lisbon have all con-tributed to a greater workload of both the CJEU and the General Court. The CJEU wants to avoid the situation where case congestion leads to growing delays by simplifying procedures and filtering appeals from the General Court. In 2013 the average duration for a preliminary reference request to be dealt with was 16.3 months and that for a direct action 24.3 months. The Court was also concerned with the increase in the number of judges asso-ciated with enlargement and a loss of its collegiate function. The House of Lords European Committee produced a report in 2011 reviewing the workload of the CJEU and supporting the Court's request for reform and more finance. There has been some reform but generally the finances have not been available to make substantial changes. The development of specialist courts such as the Civil Service Tribunal has taken some of the workload off the General Court in particular, but the possibility of a large volume of cases from the European Chemical Agency (ECHA) could further increase the workload and thus increase delays.

The General Court

The General Court was originally established under the SEA as the Court of First Instance (CFI) and came into operation in 1989. The General Court is attached to the CJEU and has a wide jurisdiction with a possible appeal to the CJEU itself on a point of law. The Treaties use the word "attach" quite deliberately. The General Court is not a separate institution. It shares not only the building in Luxembourg with the CJEU but other facilities such as the library. It appoints its own Registrar but other administrative services are shared.

The General Court is based on art.19 TEU and art.256 TFEU. There are 28 judges appointed to the court, one from each Member State. Although there are no Advocates-General specifically appointed to the General Court the need for such a role to be fulfilled is recognised. Where an Advocate-General is required in a particular case, one of the judges is requested to carry out this role. This will not happen in every case before the General Court. The court may sit in chambers of three or five judges in order to hear cases brought before it.

Like the judges appointed to the CJEU, those appointed to the General Court have a six-year term of office, which is renewable. The criteria for selection as a judge in the General Court is not so high as for the CJEU, where prospective judges must possess the ability for appointment to high judicial office. Article 254 TFEU states that for the General Court judges are to be chosen "from persons whose independence is beyond doubt and who possess the ability required for appointment to judicial office".

Jurisdiction   The initial jurisdiction of the General Court reflected one of the problems encountered by the CJEU. These were those cases that required a long examination of questions of fact. These are very time consuming and involve sifting through a great deal of evidence. There were three categories of cases that formed the original jurisdiction of the General Court:

1. Staff cases, where employees of the European Union have a dispute with regard to their employment;
2. cases brought under the European Coal and Steel Community Treaty concerned with production and prices; and
3. most importantly, competition cases brought under either art.263 TFEU or art.265 TFEU.

If these cases also contain a claim for damages, the General Court can hear that claim as part of the action. Appeals from the General Court are to the CJEU and have to be brought within two months. The appeal will only be heard on points of law and not of fact. The three grounds of appeal mirror the grounds of annulment under art.263 TFEU, namely lack of competence; breach of procedure; or infringement of Community law by the General Court.

In September 1993 there was the first major increase in the jurisdiction of the General Court since its creation in 1989. The Council extended the jurisdiction to cover all direct actions brought by private parties against the EU institutions. One of the main purposes for the extension of the jurisdiction was to permit the CJEU to reduce still further delays in hearing cases by cutting the court's case load. However, the CJEU will take on the role as the appeal court for all the cases transferred to the General Court—all cases heard by the General Court at first instance may be appealed to the CJEU on a point of law. The General Court has been recognised as a success and the Treaty of Nice allowed for the Court to hear references for preliminary ruling under art.276 TFEU after 2004. To allow for this increase in workload cases brought by staff members of the EU are now dealt with by the European Union Civil Service Tribunal with an appeal to the General Court. With the ending of the European Coal and Steel Community Treaty it may be thought that the General Court would be able to accommodate the additional workload associated with the enlargement of the EU. However, even with the increase in the number of judges in the General Court it still struggles to cope with the increased number of cases within a reasonable period. Suggestions have been made to appoint Advocate-Generals specifically to the General Court or to establish another specialist tribunal under art.257 TFEU dealing with intellectual property cases but these have so far been rejected due to budget restraints.

The EU Civil Service Tribunal   The Treaty of Nice made provision for the establishment of judicial panels to deal with litigation in specific areas and the Civil Service Tribunal was set up in 2005. This specialist court adjudicates in disputes between the EU and its civil servants. There are seven judges in the Tribunal sitting in chambers of three for a normal hearing or a chamber of five or the full court if the point of law before them is considered sufficiently important. Their decisions can be appealed to the General Court on questions of law only.

Court of Auditors

There has been such a Court since the EU was established although it is not a court in the traditional sense as it has no judicial capacity but has an auditing/accountancy role. In the Maastricht Treaty in 1992 it was upgraded to the status of an EU institution due to the need to monitor the large budgets now controlled by the Union. The TFEU still has a Court of Auditors but with less prestige.

Articles 285–287 TFEU detail the appointment and role of the Court. The duty of the Court of Auditors is to carry out audits of all revenue and expenditure of the Union and the bodies set up by the Union. It must provide the Parliament and the Council with a statement that transactions have been legally made and that the accounts produced are accurate. At the end of the financial year the Court of Auditors has to draw up an annual report that is presented to the other Community institutions for their observations. These and the report are then published in the Official Journal. For a number of years now the Court of Auditors have signed off the Union's accounts but found serious errors or possible fraud.

There are 28 members of the Court of Auditors each serving for a six-year period that is renewable. The members of the Court elect their own President, who serves for a period of three years.

It is the Council, after consulting the Parliament, which appoints the members of the Court of Auditors. Apart from the end of their period in office or death, the Court of Justice can terminate the office of a member at the request of the Court of Auditors if he no longer fulfils the obligations of his office.

The audits carried out by the Court of Auditors can be carried out on the spot in the other institutions of the Union and the Member States. Where it takes place in the Member States they liaise with the national audit bodies, who may take part in the audit. All the EU institutions and national audit bodies must forward to the Court of Auditors any document or information it requests to carry out its task.

Advisory Institutions

There are also advisory bodies with the power to give opinions either in situations where they have been consulted by the Council or Commission or in cases where they consider it appropriate (see art.300 TFEU).

The European Economic and Social Committee was established by the original EC Treaty in 1957. A new one, the Committee of the Regions, was established by the TEU in 1992.

European Economic and Social Committee (EESC)

This is an advisory committee appointed under arts 301–304 TFEU. It consists of representatives of the various sections of economic and social life of the Community. Although the opinions of the Committee are not binding they do appear to have influence. The Commission has a very good working relationship with the Economic and Social Council Committee. The relationship with the Council has not been so well developed although attempts have been made in recent years to improve this. Since 1987 it has become a regular practice for the person holding the office of President of the Council to address the Committee on matters discussed at the European Council. This has spread to ministers from the Member State holding the Presidency to address meetings of the Committee.

Although advisory, the Commission or Council consults the Committee when it considers it appropriate in addition to those instances where it is obligatory under some articles of the Treaty for the Council or the Commission to consult the Committee. An example of this is art.91 TFEU which deals with international transport within the Union and the common rules established to implement the policy.

The total number of members of the Economic and Social Committee was said in art. 301 TFEU not to exceed 350 but in 2013 it was increased to 353 on the accession of Croatia. These are allocated to the different Member States to reflect their size, with the large countries such as France, Italy, Germany and the UK having 24 each, down to six for Luxembourg and five for

Malta. The Committee reflects three particular groups of people. The Employers Group which is made up of representatives of employers organisations and chambers of commerce; the Workers Group which represent trade unions; and a group of "Other Interests" which includes small businesses, family, environmental and similar representatives. Within these groups can be found the representatives of the various categories of economic and social activity specified in art.300 TFEU.

Committee of the Regions

This Committee consists of representatives of regional and local bodies and was said in art. 305 TFEU not to exceed a total of 350 members but this was increased to 353 with the accession of Croatia in 2013. The number of members allocated from each Member State for the Committee of the Regions is the same as for the EESC. The numbers are given in Table 2.3 below.

The individual Member States propose their members who are appointed by the Council for five years, which is renewable. The members have a duty to act independently, in the general interest of the Union. In view of the expansion of the Union's Structural Funds and the creation of a Cohesion Fund to redress the imbalance of prosperity within the Union, it is likely that this Committee will make an important contribution to the Union's decision-making.

Institutional Reforms

Apart from the European Parliament, the main institutions have remained largely unchanged since the Treaty of Rome, yet the membership and policies of the EU have been greatly enlarged. This has caused the present main institutions to creak and struggle to meet the expectations placed upon them. Reports have been produced since the mid-1970s calling for reforms to be made. The Council and the European Parliament have both funded enquiries into the state of the institutions and made recommendations. The European Parliament also produced a draft Union Treaty that specified the reforms it considered necessary. It is interesting to note the reforms called for and what actually appeared in the SEA and the TEU, both of which amended the EC Treaty. The main omission was that although reforms associated with the European Commission were identified, they were not included. Apart from voting procedures in the Council and the "co-operation" and "co-decision" procedures, the main success was the setting up of the General Court to supplement the European Court of Justice. Why has there been this delay? It is often due to the individual perspective of the relationship between the institutions held by the governments of the Member States. After all it is these governments who must agree to such reforms in the Council and obtain the ratification of the amendment in their national parliaments. The

Table 2.3 EESC & COR – Number of Representatives by Member State 2014

Member State	No of Representatives
France	24
Germany	24
Italy	24
United Kingdom	24
Poland	21
Spain	21
Romania	15
Austria	12
Belgium	12
Bulgaria	12
Czech Republic	12
Greece	12
Hungary	12
Netherlands	12
Portugal	12
Sweden	12
Croatia	9
Denmark	9
Finland	9
Ireland	9
Slovakia	9
Lithuania	9
Estonia	7
Latvia	7
Slovenia	7
Cyprus	6
Luxembourg	6
Malta	5

Source Arts 301 & 305 **TFEU** amended by the accession of Croatia in 2013

expansion in the number of Member States renewed the pressure for institutional reform and the Treaty of Amsterdam, but more importantly the Treaty of Nice, brought about some reforms but not perhaps those thought necessary by the European Parliament. However, at the Nice Inter-Governmental

Conference (IGC) a declaration was made that led to the establishment of the European Convention on the Future of Europe. This Convention had the remit to consider fundamental questions about the institutions needed by an enlarged EU and they presented a draft Constitutional Treaty that was signed by the heads of government in 2004. The problems of ratification in summer 2005 meant that this Treaty was not brought into law. Due to the failure to get a positive referendum vote in France and the Netherlands a "period of reflection" was taken to discuss future action. It was decided that the best way forward was for an amending treaty to be agreed instead of the "constitutional treaty" that had such a negative reception. The Constitutional Treaty included a reduction in the number of Commissioners so that each Member State would not automatically have a Commissioner but rather there would be limited to two-thirds of the number of Member States, based on a system of rotation. In June 2008 the first Irish referendum on the Lisbon Treaty resulted in a no vote. Following this vote a number of concessions were made to Ireland including that the number of Commissioners would not be reduced and that every Member State would nominate a Commissioner. In the October 2009 referendum the Ireland voted in favour of the Lisbon Treaty. The subsequent Treaty of Lisbon was ratified on December 1, 2009 and that is why we now have two treaties—the Treaty on European Union (TEU) and the Treaty on the Functioning of the European Union (TFEU). (See Ch.12— "TEU and Beyond", p.166.)

"True Europeans"

Although the European Commissioners see themselves as the true Europeans as they have to take an independent European view on policy, the Court of Justice of the European Union sees itself as having a very pro-European Union role. Perhaps the strongest example is the way the Court developed the principle of "Direct Effect" in the very early stages of the EU. It may also take the form of guarding its own position within the context of a unique international community as with the Laying-up Fund case in Opinion 1/76 or recognising the exclusive Union competence, and with it the European Commission role in international negotiations in the ERTA case. The final example is the CJEU decisions allowing the European Parliament to bring an action under art.263 TFEU in certain circumstances, even though at that time the Parliament was not listed as a privileged applicant under the article.

KEY CASE

CASE 294/83 PARTI ECOLOGISTE—LES VERTS V EP [1986] E.C.R. 1339
The European Parliament used its budget to make payments to political parties represented in the EP, ostensibly to reimburse expenditure incurred in information campaigns to explain the role of the parliament to the general public. In reality the payments were a contribution towards the election expenses. The EP made a Decision in October 1982 as to how the 43 million Euro budget for this purpose was to be allocated. Following the 1984 elections the EP made an allocation to those parties that were represented in the new Parliament. 'Les Verts' were a new party and they objected to how the monies were being allocated. How could they challenge the Decision? 'Les Verts' wanted a judicial review by the CJEU but the actions of the EP were not listed in art. 173 **EC** (now 263 **TFEU**) so the EP argued they could not be challenged.

Held: Although art.173 **EC** referred only to actions of the Council and the Commission that was not exhaustive. The Court had a wider obligation under art 164 **EC** (now art 19(1) **TEU**) to ensure that the rule of law was observed. When art.173 **EC** had been written the EP had no powers to bind others and this had changed. The Decision of 1982 was intended to be binding upon the political parties and therefore had legal effects. The actions of the EP were subject to review and the Decision was declared void

Commentary
The EP is now listed in art 263 **TFEU** so now it can challenge acts of the Council and the Commission by way of judicial review and its actions can be challenged. However, this case illustrates how the CJEU is influenced by policy. All courts are influenced to some extent but here the CJEU had made a decision that it 'ought' to hear this case so it ignored the clear wording of the Treaty in order to do so. The Court also used this method of interpretation in the Chernobyl case (C-70/88) to identify the right of the EP to challenge the Council.

REVISION CHECKLIST

You should now know and understand:

- [ ] **the role, functions & memberships of the European Parliament**
- [ ] **the decision making process within the European Union**
- [ ] **the relationship between the European Parliament and the Council of Ministers and the Commission**

- ☐ the role, function and membership of the Council of Ministers
- ☐ the role of the Committee of Permanent Representatives (COREPER)
- ☐ the role, function and membership of the European Court of Justice
- ☐ the role, function and membership of the General Court
- ☐ the role, function and membership of the European Economic and Social Committee and the Committee of the Regions
- ☐ the role, function and membership of the European Council

SUMMARY OF KEY CASES

Case	Court	Key Principle
C-70/88 Chernobyl case	CJEU	Court recognised the right of the EP to bring action for judicial review before it became a privileged applicant under art.263 TFEU.
C-432/04 Commission v Cresson	CJEU	Cresson's breach of obligations as a Commissioner nearly deprived her of her pension rights.
C-139/79 Maizena v Council	CJEU	See Roquette v Council below.
C-294/83 Parti Ecologiste—Les Verts v EP	CJEU	Court recognised the right of the EP to bring action for judicial review before it became a privileged applicant under art.263 TFEU.
C-138/79 Roquette v Council	CJEU	Failure to consult the EP led to annulment due to infringement of procedural requirement.

QUESTION AND ANSWER

QUESTION

Critically review the powers of the European Parliament in the light of recent treaty amendments.

ADVICE AND THE ANSWER

Points you should cover in your answer to this essay question: Introduction—The EP is the only democratic institution in the EU as it is directly elected since 1979. At that time there was the role in budget approval and the consultation procedure.

Recent treaties should be identified with the Treaty of Lisbon being the most important in the form of the TEU and the TFEU. The role played by the Maastricht, Amsterdam and Nice Treaties with the recognition that the SEA in 1986 did introduce the cooperation procedure. The recent developments have been on two fronts, namely the involvement in the legislative procedure and the appointment of the Commission.

In relation to the legislative procedure the co-decision procedure (art.294 TFEU), now called the ordinary legislative procedure, has been the most significant development as it gives the EP the right to stop EU legislation being passed unless it is content. Introduced in the TEU the policy areas covered by the co-decision procedure have been extended by all subsequent treaties including Amsterdam, Nice and now Lisbon.

With regard to the appointment of the Commission the EP has to agree to the nominated candidate for the role of President of the Commission otherwise the Council has to come forward with another candidate. Subsequently the EP has to approve the appointment on the remaining members of the Commission.

The appointment of the President of the Commission, Jean-Claude Juncker, in 2014 provided a situation where the EP interpreted art.17(7) TEU to emphasise their role. The identification by the main parties of a 'prospective President of the Commission' before the elections was used to make the European Council feel bound to nominate the candidate of the majority party in the EP.

Conclusion—The momentum from the previous treaties and the failed Constitution Treaty has been maintained by the Treaty of Lisbon.

This reflects the greater powers that had to be given to the EP in response to what has been identified as the "democratic deficit" in the EU. This strategy is likely to be followed in the future to give more powers to the EP.

Sources of Union Law

3

INTRODUCTION

For the study of any legal system the sources of law are important and this applies to the European Union. However, some of the terminology is different and that sometimes causes problems for students. It is important to understand the supremacy of the Treaties as a source of law and this is not easy from a UK perspective where there is no single document like a written constitution that the student would look to as being of greater importance than others and where international law is viewed as being a different type of law outside the scope of the courts.

PRIMARY AND SECONDARY SOURCES OF UNION LAW

The European Union is founded upon treaties. The transfer of sovereignty or powers from the Member States to the institutions of the Union is limited to specific policies and specific procedures to be found in the treaties. Thus the main treaties establishing the European Union (but originally called the European Economic Community), EURATOM, the TEU (or Maastricht Treaty), subsequently amended by the Treaties of Amsterdam and Nice and now the Treaty of Lisbon are the primary source of Union law. Wherever there is any doubt about the validity or authority of a particular measure, the lawyer should always go back to the source document, which invariably is one of the treaties. This is obviously in recognition of the international law aspect of the Union. All other sources of Union law are secondary or derived in that they originate from powers conferred on particular institutions by the treaties.

Treaties

The main treaties, listed above, set down the aims and objectives of the Union and provide a framework for legislation. The most important Treaty is the Treaty of Lisbon which is divided into two parts—the Treaty on European Union (TEU) and the Treaty on the Functioning of the European Union (TFEU). These treaties have greatly extended the original Treaty of Rome signed in 1957 which formed the then European Economic Community. There are other treaties in the sense that there has to be one whenever new members join the Union, together with an Act of Accession for that particular member. In addition there have been important amendments to the original Treaty such as the Merger Treaty (1965) and the Single European Act (SEA) (1986). However, these amend and do not replace the original Treaty. It is usual for a "consolidation edition" of the EU Treaty to be produced to make for ease of reference. All the Treaties can be found on the European Union web site.

Administrative Acts under article 289 TFEU

TREATY HIGHLIGHTER

Article 288 **TFEU** has been greatly amended by previous treaties such as the **SEA** and the **TEU**, principally to recognise the increasing role of the European Parliament. Under the article "the institutions shall adopt regulations, directives, decisions, recommendations and opinions". Recommendations and opinions are not legally binding and therefore will not be considered in detail. The **Constitutional Treaty 2004** would have simplified this by having two categories: European Laws (the current Regulations) and European Framework Laws (currently Directives) but this treaty was never ratified and so did not become law. Therefore under the **Treaty of Lisbon** the appropriate terms remain Regulations and Directives.

Regulations

Regulations are the most important derived source of Union law in that they are the chosen form when legislating for the whole Union, without going through any national channels. It is defined as "having general application, binding in its entirety and directly applicable in all member States". In the Joined Cases 16 & 17/62 *Producteurs de Fruits v Council* the Court stated that "a regulation, being essentially of a legislative nature, is applicable not to a limited number of persons, defined or identifiable, but to categories of persons viewed abstractly and in their entirety". The confusion over the term "directly applicable" is discussed with the principle of direct effect in the next chapter (see p.46).

Directives

"Directives shall be binding, as to the result to be achieved, upon each Member State to which it is addressed, but shall leave to the national authorities the choice of form and methods".

This shows that directives lay down an objective and then leave it to the individual Member State to decide how best to achieve it. In the UK this may take the form of an Act of Parliament, as with the Consumer Protection Act 1987 (implementing the European Community Directive on Liability for Defective Products 1985 (85/374/EEC)) or by one of the other methods available such as a statutory instrument. It may be that in a given situation, a Member State feels that it already has domestic legislation that meets most of the objectives set and will therefore merely introduce domestic legislation on the remainder. This does carry the hidden danger that they are mistaken and subsequent action in the national courts (Case 8/81 *Ursula Becker v Finanzamt*), or by the Commission under art.258 TFEU is necessary to enforce the obligation under the directive.

Although the form may differ between Member States, allowing for national traditions, the obligation on the Member State remains the same. Every directive specifies a time period, which is usually two years, by which time the Member State should have achieved the result required. If it has not done so, an individual may seek to enforce in their national courts any rights given to them under the directive by the principle of direct effect (Case 148/78 *Tullio Ratti v Ministero Pubblico*).

Decisions

Decisions are addressed to specific Member States, individuals or companies and are binding in their entirety upon those to whom they are addressed. They are most commonly used where the Commission has reached the conclusion that an undertaking is acting contrary to the competition policy of the Union under art.101 or 102 TFEU.

Publication and notification

Under art.296 TFEU regulations, directives and decisions must state the reasons on which they are based. In the preamble to such measures the justification or authority for them is based upon a Treaty article. They must be published in the Official Journal (art.297 TFEU). The regulation or directive will come into force on the date specified in them or if no date is given on the twentieth day following their publication. Decisions are notified to whom they are addressed and take effect upon notification.

All Union acts are numbered together with the year they were enacted. For example, a directive would appear as Council Directive 64/221, recording that it was the 221st directive of 1964. Regulations have the year at the end i.e. Council Regulation 4064/89 for a Regulation made in 1989.

The Ordinary Legislative Procedure under article 294 TFEU

There are different procedures which apply to different areas of legislation as explained in art.289 TFEU but the ordinary legislative procedure is the main one. It used to be referred to as the Co-decision Procedure although this term ever appeared in the Maastricht Treaty which introduced it. The scope of the procedure was limited initially but it gradually developed to apply to many of the areas which established the internal market. The scope of the procedure was reviewed in 1996 and, in recognition of its success, the areas of policy requiring the co-decision procedure to be used were increased by both the Treaty of Amsterdam and the Treaty of Nice.

Under the Ordinary Legislative Procedure the Commission, which has the sole power of initiative under the Treaties, sends a copy of their proposal to the Council and the European Parliament. The Parliament gives the proposal a "first reading". The Council then adopts a common position, giving its reasons for doing so to the European Parliament. The 'common position' indicates what the Member States have agreed to amongst themselves. It can provide a marker showing just how far the governments have come towards agreeing the terms of a particularly complex piece of legislation. They have a certain legal weight and are published in the EU's Official Journal. EU governments must adopt a common position before the European Parliament can begin its second reading of a particular proposal. At the second reading the Parliament has three months in which to accept the Council's common position, in which case it is adopted by the Council as legislation, or to reject it. If it does neither the Council's common position is accepted anyway. In the case of a rejection by an absolute majority of Parliament, a Conciliation Committee composed of an equal number of representatives of the Council and Parliament is convened. The Commission also takes part in the work of this Conciliation Committee, as it may alter its proposal at any time before it is adopted. The Committee has six weeks in which to approve a joint text, which if accepted by an absolute majority of Parliament and a qualified majority in the Council becomes adopted. Failure to agree such a joint text means that the proposal will fall. The periods of three months and six weeks referred to above can be extended by a maximum of one month and two weeks respectively by agreement by the Council and the Parliament. The major difference between the ordinary legislative procedure and the previous co-decision procedure is that here if the EP says no the proposal does not become law (see diagram on following page).

GENERAL PRINCIPLES OF UNION LAW

These are an important source of Union law in that they provide a useful tool for interpretation and allow Union law to be challenged on the basis that it is contrary to a general principle of EU law. They may also support a claim for damages under art.340 TFEU. Every legal jurisdiction has its own general principles, which are principles which command common assent, such as the

```
┌─────────────────────────────────────────────┐
│  Commission submits a proposal to:           │
│  The Parliament (EP) and the Council         │
└─────────────────────────────────────────────┘
```

```
┌─────────────────────────────────────────────┐
│  EP adopts its position by a majority vote   │
│  (first reading) — sent to Council —         │
└─────────────────────────────────────────────┘
```

if approved by Council — becomes adopted	if rejected by Council it adopts a common position — sent to EP

if within three months:

EP approves Council's common position or has not taken any decision — proposed 'act' becomes adopted	If EP rejects Councils common position — proposed 'act' not adopted	if EP proposes amendments (second reading) forwarded to the Council

if within three months:

the Council approves the EP amendments — the proposed 'act' adopted	the Council does not approve the EP amendments — Conciliation Committee convened

```
┌─────────────────────────────────────────────┐
│  Conciliation Committee composed of equal    │
│  members of Council or representatives and   │
│  the EP have six weeks to agree joint text   │
│  (Commission takes initiatives in order to   │
│  seek agreement)                             │
└─────────────────────────────────────────────┘
```

If agree text — goes to EP and Council — if within six weeks the EP by a majority of MEPs & the Council by qualified voting agree to joint text the proposed 'act' adopted. If they do not do so the proposed 'act' fails.	If fail to agree text then the proposed 'act' fails.

right to natural justice. The CJEU has justified its action in identifying general principles of EU law by referring to three articles in the Treaty. Article 19 TEU states that the Court shall ensure that in the interpretation and application of the Treaty the law is observed. Second, in art.263 TFEU the grounds for annulment include "infringement of the Treaty, or of any rule of law relating to its application". In both of these references "law" must refer to something outside the Treaties themselves. Lastly, art.340(2) TFEU, which is concerned with non-contractual liability, expressly provides that the liability of the Union is based on the "general principles common to the laws of the Member States".

The CJEU has derived general principles of Union law from the Treaties and from the legal systems of the Member States. For example, art.7 EC (now repealed and replaced by art. 18 TFEU) which prohibited discrimination based on nationality was used by the CJEU as the foundation for a general principle which forbids arbitrary discrimination on any ground. Article 6 TEU contains a strong statement in relation to fundamental rights of citizens of the EU. When looking at the legal systems of the Member States the CJEU is not looking for a principle to be common to all of them before it may be adopted. It is sufficient if it is generally accepted. Whatever the factual origin of the principle, it is applied by the CJEU as a general principle of Union law. The most important examples of general principles are as follows.

Proportionality

A public authority may not impose obligations on a citizen except to the extent to which they are strictly necessary in the public interest to attain the purpose of the measure. If the burdens imposed are clearly out of proportion to the object in view, the measure will be annulled if challenged in the courts. This principle, derived from German law, is important in economic law where levies or charges are involved. In the *Skimmed-Milk Powder* case (Case 114/76) the Commission needed to reduce a surplus of skimmed-milk powder in the Union by requiring animal feed producers to incorporate it into their products in place of soya. Unfortunately this also meant that the price of the feed would be increased by three fold. The CJEU declared the regulation concerned was invalid, partly because it discriminated against some farmers and partly because it was against the principle of proportionality. The requirement placed on the producers was not necessary in order to diminish the surplus.

Protection of Legitimate Expectations

This is another principle derived from German law, whereby Union measures must not violate the legitimate expectations of those concerned, unless there is an overriding matter of public interest. In Case 78/74 *Deuka v EVGF*, the CJEU interpreted a Commission regulation setting the denaturing premiums for common wheat so as to protect the legitimate expectations of the processors.

Non-Discrimination

As was mentioned above this was derived from the Treaty arts 7 EC (now art 18 TFEU)) and 157 TFEU. Art.18 TFEU prohibits discrimination on the grounds of nationality and art 157 TFEU provides for equal pay and equal treatment in the workplace. However, the CJEU has gone beyond these specific provisions to hold that there is a general principle of non-discrimination (see *Deuka v EVGF* above). In Case 20/71 *Sabbatini v European Parliament*, Sabbatini, who was employed by the European Parliament, successfully used the principle against her employer's staff regulations when she lost an expatriation allowance on her marriage. In Case 130/75 *Prais v Council* the principle was extended to discrimination on the grounds of religion.

KEY CASE

CASE 20/71 SABBATINI V EUROPEAN PARLIAMENT

Facts: Miss Luisa Bertoni, an Italian national, entered the service of the European Parliament on January 1, 1960. On her appointment she was awarded an expatriation allowance as prescribed by the Staff Regulations as it is granted in particular to officials who are not and have never been nationals of the State in whose European territory the place where they are employed is situated. On November 4, 1970 Miss Bertoni married Sereno Sabbatini, who was not an official of the Union. On November 17, 1970 she was informed that consequent upon her marriage she would lose, as from December 1, 1970, her right to an expatriation allowance. On February 15, 1971 Miss Sabbatini asked for the decision to be reviewed but this was refused as the Staff Regulations did not allow this. Consequently Miss Sabbatini brought a challenge before the Court of Justice.

Held: 'It is thus clear that the provision the validity of which is contested does in fact create a difference of treatment as between male and female officials inasmuch as it renders the retention of the expatriation allowance conditional upon the acquisition of the status of head of household within the meaning of the Staff Regulations'. The Court annulled the decision of the EP to withdraw the expatriation allowance.

Commentary: In this case the Court established sex equality as a general principle of law. This principle has been further developed in the case law of the Court but more importantly in the articles of the Treaties.

Protection of Fundamental Rights

In Case 29/69 *Stauder v Ulm* the CJEU recognised that the protection of such rights was inspired by the constitutional traditions common to all the Member States. The protection of fundamental rights was therefore enshrined in the general principles of Union law and thus protected by the CJEU. Stauder had been required to give his name when he applied for cheap butter under a Union scheme. Case 11/70 *Internationale Handelsgesellschaft* took the recognition of this principle a step further as the German courts were unhappy with the Union's protection of fundamental rights in contrast with that provided by the German basic law.

KEY CASE

CASE 11/70 INTERNATIONALE HANDELSGESELLSCHAFT

In this case the attempt to control the common agriculture policy led to the introduction of a system whereby exports were permitted only if the exporter first obtained an export licence. To obtain a licence a deposit had to be paid which would be forfeited if the level of exports did not happen. The applicants complained that this was contrary to fundamental rights protected by the German constitution.

Held: The CJEU held that the matter had to be approached from Union law and not German law but came to the conclusion that no fundamental right had been violated.

Commentary: This case is one of the early cases that came before the CJEU concerning fundamental rights and the need for proportionality when applying EU policies. It made the Court realise that the protection of fundamental rights found in Member States had to be mirrored in the Union.

(See also Case 44/79 *Hauer v Land Rheinland-Pfalz*.) There was a similar discussion in Italy in Case 33/84 *Fragd v Amministrazione delle Finanze dello Stato*. Article 6 TEU now gives specific recognition of this general principle. There is a Charter of Fundamental Rights of the EU and by art.6 TEU this now has legal force and "shall have the same legal value as the Treaties". However, by Protocol 30 the Charter does not extend to Poland and the UK unless those Member States have specifically extended the rights in their national laws. There has been some dispute as to the extent of this 'opt out', especially when EU law is being applied.

Procedural Rights

The main procedural rights are the right to be heard and the right to due process.

(a) Right to be Heard

Based on English law this principle requires that a person whose interests are perceptively affected by a decision taken by a public authority must be give the opportunity to make his point of view known (Case 17/74 *Transocean Marine Paint v Commission*).

(b) Right to Due Process

This right follows on from the duty of those exercising authority to give reasons for a decision. In Case 222/84 *Johnston v Chief Constable of the Royal Ulster Constabulary* a certificate issued by the Secretary of State for Northern Ireland sought to provide exclusive evidence that the derogation from Union obligations under Directive 76/207 was on the grounds of national security. Mrs Johnston claimed that she had been subject to sex discrimination by her employer, contrary to Union law. The CJEU held that the action of the Secretary of State was contrary to the requirement of judicial control, recognised as a general principle by the Member States.

JUDGMENTS OF THE EUROPEAN COURT OF JUSTICE AND THE GENERAL COURT

Although these courts do not follow the system of binding precedent found in common law jurisdictions such as England, they do accept the importance of certainty as a principle of law. Therefore the judgments of previous cases before these courts do affect future cases. After all the CJEU is the final arbiter of Union law. They are thus a source of Union law when an individual is seeking to identify what the law is. For example, there have been certain cases which appear to have no obvious connection with either the Treaty or legislative act, but which have been used by the Court of Justice of the European Union to develop the principle of direct effect. This is discussed below.

Methods of interpretation

When called upon to identify what the law is the CJEU has to interpret the treaties, administrative acts and other such generic sources of law. To assist in this process the CJEU has evolved a number of methods of interpretation, which other courts can utilise when dealing with questions of Union law. The methods used by the CJEU have been influenced by the traditions of the

Member States, notably France and Germany. However, there are special problems facing the Court, including the linguistic one that there are twenty-four official versions of a text. This principle of linguistic equality has affected the Court as it has developed a particular "European Union way" of interpretation.

The main "tools" of interpretation used by the Court are:

(a) teleological, which requires the judge to look to the purpose or object of the text before him;

(b) the contextual approach, which involves the court placing the provision within its context and interpreting it in relation to other provisions of Union law;

(c) historical interpretation, which requires an attempt to ascertain the subjective intention of the author by looking at documentation available to the court;

(d) literal interpretation, which is familiar to any judge, but with Union law once its literal meaning has been identified it is then necessary to apply the teleological or contextual approach.

The Court appears to favour the first two methods of interpretation, teleological and contextual, as they assist in the development of the Union towards the objectives listed in the first part of the Lisbon Treaty.

REVISION CHECKLIST

You should now know and understand:

☐ the importance of the Treaties as the primary source of EU law

☐ the types of administrative acts under art.288 TFEU

☐ the definition of a Regulation, a Directive and a Decision

☐ the requirements of the Ordinary Legislative Procedure in art.294 TFEU

☐ the use of General Principles as a source of EU law and the important role they play

☐ the meaning of general principles such as—Proportionality, Protection of legitimate expectations, Non-discrimination, Protection of fundamental rights and Procedural rights

☐ the main "tools" of interpretation used by the CJEU Court

SUMMARY OF KEY CASES

Case	Court	Key Principle
C-78/74 Deuka v EVGF	CJEU	Application of general principle of 'legitimate expectations'.
C-33/84 Fragd v Amministrazione delle Finanze dello Stato.	CJEU	Italian constitutional court raised concerns about judgement of CJEU.
C-44/79 Hauer v Land Rheinland-Pfalz.)	CJEU	CJEU uses traditions of national courts to identify EU protection of human rights.
C-11/70 Internationale Handelsgesellschaft	CJEU	German constitutional court stated that if EU law was in breach of German Constitution it would not be applied.
C-222/84 Johnston v Chief Constable of the Royal Ulster Constabulary	CJEU	The Chief Constable is an 'emanation of the state' and the measures to prohibit discrimination were contrary to EU law.
C-130/75 Prais v Council	CJEU	Freedom of religion recognised as a general principle of EU law.
C-16 & 17/62 Producteurs de Fruits v Council	CJEU	'What distinguishes a Regulation is not the greater or lesser extent of its application...but the fact that its provisions apply impersonally in objective situations..'
C-20/71 Sabbatini v European Parliament	CJEU	Established sex equality as a general principle of EU law.
C-114/76 Skimmed-Milk Powder case	CJEU	Application of the general principle of 'proportionality' to stop discrimination in animal feeds.

C-29/69 Stauder v Ulm	CJEU	CJEU recognised that EU law was capable of prejudicing fundamental human rights and that EU law would protect such rights.
C-17/74 Transocean Marine Paint v Commission	CJEU	CJEU recognised the right to a hearing as a general principle—derived from English law.
C-148/ 78 Tullio Ratti v Ministero Pubblico	CJEU	Ratti could rely on a Directive that had direct effect but which the Member State had failed to implement.
C-8/81 Ursula Becker v Finanzamt	CJEU	Becker could enforce a VAT Directive that had not been implemented by the German authorities.

QUESTION AND ANSWER

QUESTION

What general principles of law have been developed in the EU? How do they assist the individual?

ADVICE AND THE ANSWER

Introduction—all legal systems have developed general principles of law to incorporate into law fundamental principles which may be taken for granted. Sometimes they may appear formally as with the principle of equality and non-discrimination found in the Union treaties. The European Court of Justice has developed many principles which have been derived from the law of the Member States or from other sources to provide general principles of Community law.

Examples of the main general principles should then be reviewed including:

Protection of fundamental rights—Case 29/69 *Stauder v Ulm*
Non-discrimination—Case 20/71 *Sabbatini v European Parliament*

Proportionality—the *Skimmed-Milk Powder* Case 114/76
Protection of legitimate expectations—Case 78/74 *Deuka v EVGF*
Right to be heard—Case 17/74 *Transocean Marine Paint v Commission*

The assistance that is provided for the individual is that they can provide rights which the courts will recognise when deciding questions of Union law. For example if the action is under art.263 TFEU the breach of a general principle could be a ground for declaring a Community measure such as a Decision void. If the matter is before a national court, which can not declare a Union law void, the general principle may influence the enforcement of the Union law or make the national court use the preliminary ruling procedure under art.267 TFEU to clarify the law.

EU and National Law

4

. . . .

SUPREMACY OF UNION LAW INTRODUCTION

In the UK the legislation passed by Parliament has been given greater importance than any other source of law. However, the EU is based on principles of international law and gives greater priority to the international agreements or treaties entered into by sovereign countries. How European law has dealt with the issues arising from this relationship is the subject of this chapter.

The relationship between Union and national law was established in the case of *Costa v ENEL*, one of the earliest cases to come before the European Court of Justice.

KEY CASE

CASE 6/64 COSTA V ENEL

In Case 6/64 *Costa v ENEL* an action was brought in Italy against the nationalised National Electricity Board (ENEL) over a bill of 1,950 lire which then amounted to less than 1 Euro. Mr Costa claimed that he was not obliged to pay the bill as the nationalisation legislation had infringed Italian and EC law. A reference was made for a preliminary ruling by the Italian court under art.267 **TFEU**. The Italian government argued that such a reference was "absolutely inadmissible" because the national court had to apply national law.

Held: The CJEU rejected that argument in a passage that has been repeated on many subsequent occasions.

"By contrast with ordinary international treaties, the **EEC Treaty** has created its own legal system which ... became an integral part of the legal systems of the Member States and which their courts are bound to apply. By creating a Community of unlimited duration, having its own institutions, its own personality, its own legal capacity ... and real powers stemming from a limitation of sovereignty or a transfer of powers from the States to the Community, the Member States have limited their sovereign rights, albeit within limited fields, and thus created a body of law which binds both their nationals and themselves ... It follows ... that the law stemming from the Treaty, an independent source of law, could not, because of its special and original nature, be over-ridden by domestic legal provisions, however framed, without being deprived of its character as Community law and without the legal basis of the Community itself being called into question."

Commentary: This important case set the precedent with regard to the relationship between national and EU law. To the disappointment of the Member States, who argued that the procedures in the Treaties for an enforcement action by the Commission or another Member State should be used, the Court created a power that has allowed individuals to enforce EU law in their national courts.

Union Law Prevails

Thus on the basis of a case involving very little money the principle was established that where there is conflict between Union law and national law it is Union law which is to prevail. If it was otherwise "the obligations under the Treaty could be called into question" by any subsequent national legislation the government of a Member State passed through its legislature. *Costa v ENEL* developed this basic principle that had been set down in Case 26/62 *Van Gend en Loos v Nederlanse Tariefcommissie* one year earlier.

Although the Treaties do not expressly mention the principle of supremacy, a number of provisions require it. For the CJEU the position is unequivocal. By creating the Union the Member States consented to transfer to it certain of their powers and to restrict their sovereign rights. The CJEU case- law is directed at the national courts who apply the law in the cases which come before them and apply effective remedies. Thus we have the statement in Case 92/78 *Simmenthal v Commission* that the provisions of Union law "are an integral part of, and take precedence in, the legal order applicable in the territory of each of the Member States".

Full recognition was given in the UK to the principle of supremacy in Case 213/89 *R. v Secretary of State for Transport, Ex p. Factortame Ltd.*

KEY CASE

CASE C-213/89 R. V SECRETARY OF STATE FOR TRANSPORT, EX P. FAC-TORTAME (NO. 2)

A number of cases were brought by Factortame as a result of the government passing the **Merchant Shipping Act 1988** and the **Merchant Shipping (Registration of Fishing Vessels) Regulations 1988**. This legislation had been passed following criticism that a number of

UK registered fishing boats were in fact operated by Spanish fishermen. This legislation required a nationality link for registration of vessels so that ownership would remain in British hands. The CJEU, in response to a request for a preliminary reference under art.267 **TFEU**, restated the relationship between national and Community law. Lord Bridge in his judgment in the House of Lords stated: "If the supremacy within the EC of Community law over the national law of the Member States was not always inherent in the **EEC Treaty** it was certainly well established in the jurisprudence of the Court of Justice long before the UK joined the Community. Thus, whatever limitation of its sovereignty Parliament accepted when it enacted the European Communities Act 1972 was entirely voluntary". Therefore, Union law will prevail over inconsistent UK legislation, even where that legislation has been enacted by Parliament subsequent to the entry into force of the Union rule.

Commentary: This case had fundamental repercussions for UK constitutional law as never before had an act of parliament been set aside and not applied. The CJEU looked to earlier cases such as *Simmenthal* (1978) to state that it was for national courts to ensure that rights which individuals derived from the direct effect of EU law were protected.

In *Equal Opportunities Commission v Secretary of State for Employment* [1995] 1 A.C. 1 the House of Lords held that the **Employment Protection (Consolidation) Act 1978** requirements regarding qualifying periods of employment were contrary to European law.

Incorporation of Union law into National Law

When a State joins the European Union it is obliged to reconcile its constitution with Union membership. It does this by making provision for the application of Union law within its territory and for the supremacy of Union law over national law. How the State will achieve this will depend upon its conception of international law, as there are two possibilities: namely monist and dualist.

CHECKPOINT

Monist Approach

The monist conception is that international law and national law are both part of one legal structure, even though they operate in different spheres. In such countries there is no reason why the national courts should not apply international law, provided that the appropriate constitutional procedures have been gone through to receive them into the national system. In cases where there is a conflict with national law, monist countries usually recognise the supremacy of treaty provisions, as for example happens in France and the Netherlands.

CHECKPOINT

Dualist Approach

The dualist conception is that international law and national law are two fundamentally different structures. Therefore in such countries national courts can never apply international treaties unless domestic legislation makes this possible. The UK is a dualist country and therefore the **European Communities Act 1972** was specifically enacted to make provision for UK membership of the Community. Lord Denning made clear in *McWhirter v Attorney-General* [1972] C.M.L.R. 882 that without this Act the **EC Treaty** and Community legislation would have been binding on the UK in international law but would have had no effect internally. Sections 2 and 3 of the **European Communities Act 1972** achieve this purpose.

DIRECT EFFECT

This important principle was created by the CJEU and follows on from the principle of supremacy of Union law. It is a novel concept and can appear complex in the way it applies to particular Union provisions. If a legal provision is said to be directly effective, it means that it grants individual rights that must be upheld by the national courts. There are two initial requirements that have to be satisfied as the provision must be part of the legal order and its terms must be appropriate to confer rights on individuals. There is thus a close link between supremacy of Union law and direct effect as they both flow from the nature of the Union. In the important case of Case 26/62 *Van Gend en Loos v Nederlanse Tariefcommissie*, the CJEU identified 'a new legal order' that has had a fundamental impact on the subsequent development of EU law.

Case 26/62 Van Gend en Loos v Nederlanse Tariefcommissie

Facts: Van Gend imported chemicals from Germany into the Nether-lands. In 1959 a Dutch law was passed which imposed a duty on some imported chemicals. This was contrary to art.30 **TFEU** which required Member States to refrain from introducing new duties or raising existing ones on imports between the States. Van Gend objected to paying the duty and a reference was made under art.67 **TFEU** to the CJEU to ascertain whether the duty on the chemicals was prohibited.

Held: The conclusion reached by the CJEU was that:

"the Community constitutes a new legal order of international law for the benefit of which the states have limited their sover-eign rights, albeit within limited fields, and the subjects of which comprise not only the Member States but also their nationals. Independently of the legislation of the Member States, Commu-nity law therefore not only imposes obligations on individuals but is also intended to confer upon them rights which become part of their legal heritage".

Commentary: The development of the principle of direct effect in this case and *Costa v ENEL* (above) provided a means by which individuals could enforce their rights under EU law in their national courts without the lengthy procedures of seeking the Commission to bring the Member State into line.

Direct Effect and Member States

The judgment in *Van Gend* was not the one that the Member States had argued for. As far as they were concerned if there was a breach of a Union obligation the Treaty provided for action to be taken by the Commission under art.258 **TFEU**, or by another Member State under art.259 **TFEU**. These procedures have the advantage for the Member State that they take a long time to come before the CJEU and, until the Maastricht Treaty, did not carry any real sanction. The statements in *Van Gend*, clearly giving the individual who is affected by Union law the equipment to take action in his national courts, ensure that the Member States observe their obligations.

Conditions for Direct Effect

The principle of direct effect is a very powerful one and the CJEU has taken the view that it has to be limited by being interpreted restrictively. The judgment in *Van Gend* pointed out that art.25 EC (ex 12 EC) was ideally adapted to have direct effect on the legal relations between the Member

States and their subjects. The Court did this by establishing what are now recognised as the conditions which must apply if direct effect is to be enforced.

The conditions which must apply if direct effect is to be enforced are:

1. the provision must be clear and unambiguous;
2. it must be unconditional; and
3. its operation must not be dependent on further action being taken by Union or national authorities.

The principle of direct effect has been applied to all the legally binding sources of Union law. Whether or not a provision has direct effect is a question of interpretation of Union law. In this way the CJEU seeks to ensure uniformity throughout the European Union.

Direct effect of Treaty provisions

The CJEU established in *Van Gend en Loos* that Treaty articles that impose on Member States an obligation to abstain from something, such as levying duties under art.30 TFEU have direct effect. In Case 57/67 *Firma Alfons Lütticke GmbH v Hauptzollamt Sarrelouis* [1971] C.M.L.R. 674 a preliminary reference was made asking if art.110 TFEU, which deals with taxation, had direct effect. The Court used the familiar phrases when it stated, "The first paragraph of Article 110 TFEU contains a prohibition against discrimination, constituting a clear and unconditional obligation". There being no discretion left to Member States, it concluded that art.110 TFEU produced direct effects and creates individual rights of which national courts must take account. See also Case 43/75 *Defrenne v Sabena (No.2)*.

Direct effect of Regulations

Under art.288 TFEU regulations have general application and are binding in their entirety and directly applicable in all Member States. The term used in the article is "directly applicable" and not "direct effect", although as the CJEU often uses the terms inconsistently there is often confusion as to the difference in meaning. Direct applicability is not the same as direct effect, as the conditions or test mentioned above still has to be satisfied if direct effect is to be applied. Direct applicability means that the national courts must apply a regulation whenever their contents grants rights to individuals or impose obligations on them. In the *Politi* judgment (Case 43/71 *Politi v Ministry for Finance of the Italian Republic*) the Court held that "by reason of their nature and their function in the system of the sources of Community law, regulations have direct effect and are, as such, capable of creating individual rights which national courts must protect". The resulting enforcement of his rights by the individual is the same whether the regulation is said to be directly applicable or directly effective.

In Case 93/71 *Orsolina Leonesio v Ministero dell'agricoltura e foreste* an Italian farmer claimed a subsidy for slaughtering a cow under Community regulations. The Italian government refused on the basis that under the Italian Constitution national legislation had to be enacted before they could do so. The CJEU held that regulations become part of the national legal system and the direct applicability under art.288 TFEU cannot be hindered by national practices. There are instances where regulations do require further legislation, such as in the form of directives. In these circumstances the condition that the provision must not be dependent on further action being taken cannot be satisfied.

Direct effect of Decisions

In Case 9/70 *Franz Grad v Finanzamt Traunstein* the CJEU held that Decisions could have vertical direct effect:

> "the provisions according to which decisions are binding in their entirety on those to whom they are addressed enables the question to be put whether the obligation created by the decisions can only be invoked by the Community institutions against the addressee or whether such a right may possibly be exercised by all those who have an interest in the fulfilment of this obligation".

The answer given by the Court was that all those with an interest should have the right.

Direct effect of Directives

In contrast to the direct applicability of regulations, art.288 TFEU states that directives are addressed to Member States and are binding as to the result to be achieved. The Member States have argued that this wording means that directives cannot be directly effective because they cannot satisfy the conditions. This view was supported by the Conseil d'Etat in *Minister of the Interior v Cohn-Bendit* [1980] 1 C.M.L.R. 543. The argument was that if the choice is left to the Member States as to the form and method to achieve the obligation, they must require further action in the form of domestic legislation required. The CJEU has not accepted this argument. The effectiveness (l'effet utile) of a directive would be weakened if the nationals of a Member State that had failed to implement a directive, or had implemented it wrongly, were denied the rights contained in the directive by the national court. This was stated in *Grad*, which although concerned with a Community Decision, developed the principle that was closely repeated in Case 41/74 *Yvonne Van Duyn v Home Office* that did involve a directive. (See now Case 91/92 *Paola Faccini Dori v Recreb Srl*.)

KEY CASE

CASE 41/74 YVONNE VAN DUYN V HOME OFFICE

Facts: The principle in *Van Duyn* was **Directive 64/221** concerning restriction on the admission and movement of aliens that required interpretation. Miss Van Duyn, a Dutch national, sought a declaration that the UK government was wrong to deny her admission to take up employment with the Church of Scientology, a sect which the government considered undesirable.

Held: On a preliminary reference under art.267 **TFEU**, the CJEU held that the Directive was directly effective because it "imposes on a Member State a precise obligation which does not require the adoption of any further measure on the part of either the Union institutions or of the Member States and which leaves them, in relation to its implementation, no discretionary powers". Thus the conditions for direct effect were satisfied, although on the facts of the case it agreed that the UK government could exclude her.

Commentary: The UK government had argued in this case that the Directive could not have 'direct effect' on the basis of the definition given in the Treaties. However, although this argument was not accepted the political nature of government actions resulted in the Court accepting that in the circumstances of the case she could be stopped from exercising her rights under the Directive.

In Case 148/78 Criminal proceedings against Tullio Ratti the CJEU took the opportunity to refine its arguments for direct effect of directives. "A Member State which has not adopted the implementing measures required by a directive in the prescribed period may not rely, as against individuals, on its own failure to perform the obligations which the directive entails". If it was the government that had not fulfilled its obligations arising from the Directive, it is against the government that rights arising from the Directive can be enforced. In Case 8/81 *Ursula Becker v Finanzamt Munster-Innenstadt*, a German credit broker successfully claimed the benefit of a provision of the sixth VAT Directive against the German VAT authorities as they had failed to implement the Directive. In the important case of Case 271/91 *Marshall v Southampton and South West Hampshire AHA* the UK government had failed to properly implement the Equal Treatment Directive 76/207, which was held to be directly effective.

Vertical and horizontal direct effect

The articles of the Treaty and regulations have been held by the CJEU as being capable of giving both horizontal and vertical direct effect. Vertical effect means that an individual can invoke the obligation arising from the provision against the Member State before a national court. Horizontal effect means that an individual can invoke the obligation arising from the provision against another individual before the national court. It was also made clear in the Marshall judgment that there was no question of a directive having horizontal direct effect.

CASE 271/91 MARSHALL V SOUTHAMPTON AND SOUTH WEST HAMPSHIRE AHA

Facts: Mrs Marshall was employed by the Southampton Area Health Authority when she was dismissed because she had reached the age of 62, the Authority's retirement age for females.

Held: The CJEU accepted that this was contrary to **Equal Treatment Directive 76/207.** As the Area Health Authority was an "emanation of the State", Mrs Marshall succeeded in her action.

Commentary: Although the Court accepted the principle that Directives could not impose obligations on an individual (horizontal effect) here there was an employer who was an 'emanation of the state' (vertical effect) so it could be enforced. This is also illustrated by Case 188/89 *Foster v British Gas* where the employer was the pre-privatised Gas Board. In contrast Mrs Duke, who was employed by a public company, GEC Reliance Ltd, did not succeed because she was requesting horizontal effect to enforce the Directive against another individual, albeit a company. (See *Duke v GEC Reliance* [1988] AC 618). The principle is therefore, that unless the individual is able to show that there is some relationship with the State the principle of direct effect will not apply even if all three conditions mentioned above can be fulfilled (see *Webb v EMO Air Cargo (UK) Ltd* [1993] 1 W.L.R. 49).

In a number of cases Advocates-Generals have called on the Court to abolish the distinction between vertical and horizontal direct effect of directives. In

Case 91/92 *Faccini Dori v Recreb Srl* (1995) the CJEU refused to follow this path. In this case the Court found that the relevant provisions of the directive were unconditional and sufficiently precise, but stated that if the Community wished to enact obligations between individuals with immediate effect it could do so by adopting regulations. See the comments of the Advocate-General in Case C-104/09 *Roca Álvarez v Sesa Start España ETT SA* at para.55.

Every Directive involves a time-scale for implementation. This period, normally two years, is to give the government of the Member State time to formulate and pass the appropriate domestic measure. Until this period has elapsed the Directive cannot, as was confirmed in *Ratti* (see above), have direct effect. Ratti ran a business in Italy selling solvents and varnishes. The Union had adopted two Directives specifying the labelling and packaging of these products. Italy had not implemented the Directives but Ratti had complied with them with regard to his products. Unfortunately for him, the domestic legislation in Italy set other requirements that he had breached and he was prosecuted before the Italian court. A preliminary reference was made to the CJEU which held that as the time for the implementation of one of the Directives had passed it was directly effective thus providing Ratti with a defence. The other Directive still had time to be implemented and therefore could not be directly effective until that time had expired.

In Case 208/90 *Emmott v Minister for Social Welfare*, Mrs Emmott brought an action against the Irish Minister for Social Welfare on the basis that she received less benefit than a man would have done in equivalent circumstances. Directive 79/7 should have been implemented by 1984 but was not implemented in Ireland until 1988. Mrs Emmott's action in 1987 followed a previous case before the CJEU where it had declared that the Directive had direct effect. The vertical relationship between herself and the Irish government satisfied the case law of the Court. The Irish government, however, claimed that her action was statute barred because it had not been brought within the three months required by Irish law for judicial review. The Court held that Union law precludes the competent national authorities from relying on national procedural rules relating to time limits to stop an action by one of its citizens seeking to enforce a right that Member State has failed to transpose into its domestic legal system. The time limit does not run until the date when the national implementing legislation is correctly adopted.

Indirect Effect-Von Colson principle
If a Community act cannot satisfy the three conditions for direct effect, the individual cannot seek to have any right arising from it enforced in the national courts. This is what happened in the *Von Colson* and *Harz* cases.

CASE 14/83 VON COLSON AND KAMANN V LAND NORDRHEIN-WESTFALEN AND CASE 79/83 HARZ V DEUTSCHE TRADAX GMBH

Facts: Case 14/83 *Von Colson and Kamann v Land Nordrhein-Westfalen* and Case 79/83 *Harz v Deutsche Tradax GmbH*—when women sought remedies in the German courts for unlawful discrimination. They claimed that this was contrary to the Equal Treatment Directive 1976. On a preliminary reference the CJEU was asked whether art.6 of the Directive had direct effect.

Held: The Court did not restrict itself to the question whether there was vertical or horizontal direct effect. Instead it used art.4(3) **TEU** which requires Member States to "take all appropriate measures to ensure fulfilment of their Community obligations". Therefore even if the principle of direct effect does not apply, the courts in the Member States are required to interpret national legislation specifically passed to implement the Union act to comply with Community law.

Commentary: This case illustrates the determination of the CJEU to be creative so as to ensure that wherever possible an individual can enforce a right given to them by EU law.

In *Litster v Forth Dry Dock & Engineering Co Ltd* [1990] 1 A.C. 546, the House of Lords interpreted the Transfer of Undertakings (Protection of Employment) Regulation 1981 in such a way as to give effect to the Directive 77/187. This was because it was for the purpose of implementing the Directive that the domestic Regulation had been introduced. In this way the House of Lords was using the *Von Colson* principle to give effect not only to the Directive but also the subsequent interpretation by the CJEU of the Directive in Case 101/87 *Bork International v Forening af Arbejdsledere I Danmark*.

In Case 106/89 *Marleasing SA v La Comercial Internacional de Alimentacion SA*, the *Von Colson* principle was taken a stage further when the CJEU held that the principle could be applied even if the necessary national legislation had not been introduced to comply with the Directive. However, the CJEU has limited the *Von Colson* principle with regard to criminal prosecutions, if this would make the accused guilty where he would otherwise have been acquitted (see Case 80/86 *Officer van Justitie v Koplinghuis Nijmegen* and Case 168/95 *Criminal proceedings against Luciano Arcaro*).

In the case of *Mangold v Helm* (C-144/04) a 56 year old entered into an eight month fixed term contract of employment with Helm, a German Lawyer. He subsequently challenged the contract on the grounds that it was contrary to Directive 2000/78/EC. The Directive was not due to be transposed into national law until December 2003 at the earliest so the German government argued that it could not have legal effect until that date. The CJEU enforced the Directive not by direct effect but by stating that the Directive was fulfilling the general principle of EU law relating to non-discrimination.

Direct effect and claims for damages

In Case 479/93 *Francovich v Italian State* the CJEU extended the impact of the law regarding directives. "Community law lays down a principle according to which a Member State is liable to make good damage to individuals caused by a breach of Community law for which it is responsible".

KEY CASE

CASE C-6 & 90/90 FRANCOVICH V ITALIAN STATE

Facts: Under a Council Directive aimed at protecting employees in the event of the insolvency of their employers, Member States were required to ensure that payment of employees' outstanding claims arising from the employment relationship and relating to pay was guaranteed. Unfortunately, the Italian government had not set up any Italian system to act as a guarantor in these circumstances, hence his claim against them. His insolvent employers owed Mr Francovich six million lire. As he was unable to enforce a judgment against them, he brought an action against the Italian government for compensation.

Held: Francovich succeeded in obtaining damages. The CJEU held that 'the full effectiveness of Community rules would be undermined if individuals were unable to recover damages where their rights were infringed by a breach of EU law attributable to a Member State'. Therefore damages are available against the State for failure to implement EU directives, if three conditions are met: (a) the Directive must confer rights on individuals; (b) the contents of those rights must be identifiable in the wording of the measure and (c) there must be a causal link between the damage suffered and the failure to implement the Directive.

Commentary: This case should be seen initially as a further development by the Court to assist those claimants who could not use the principle of direct effect in order to end force a right under a Directive. This development of state liability provided another impetus to make Member States fulfil their obligations with regard to implementing Directive. The conditions identified in Francovich have been redefined in the case of C-46/93 *Brasserie du Pecheur SA v Germany* and case C-48/93 *R. v Secretary of State for Transport, Ex p. Factortame Ltd* which were held together by the CJEU. (See below.)

Limits for damages   Case 271/91 *Marshall v Southampton and South West Hampshire AHA* followed a successful action by Mrs Marshall against her employer under the Equal Treatment Directive. Under UK enacting legislation there was a limit imposed on the compensation payable for sex discrimination and no interest was allowed on this sum. The CJEU in this second case rejected the UK government's argument that limits on compensation were matters for national law. Article 6 of the Directive was directly effective and therefore such compensation had to be "adequate" to make good the loss sustained by the individual as a result of the wrongful discrimination. In computing the amount of compensation, interest should be included from the date of the discrimination.

In the Cases 46/93 and 48/93 *Brasserie du Pecheur* and *Factortame (No.4)* judgment the CJEU stated that the principles in *Francovich* applied whether it was an act or omission by the organ of the state that had caused the breach. If the three conditions were met the national court could award exemplary damages if such damages could be awarded in similar claims founded on domestic law. National legislation, which generally limited the damage for which reparation could be granted, was not compatible with Union Law.

KEY CASE

CASE C-282/10 DOMINGUEZ V CENTRE INFORMATIQUE DU CENTRE OUEST ATLANTIQUE, PRÉFET DE RÉGION CENTRE

Ms Dominguez was involved in an accident on the journey between her home and her place of work in November 2005. She was subsequently absent from work from November 3, 2005 until January 7, 2007. When her employer subsequently refused to pay her 22.5 days' paid leave in respect of that period she brought a claim before the French courts seeking compensation of €1970 in lieu. Ms Dominguez argues that an accident on the journey to or from work is a work-related accident and is covered by the same arrangements as a work-related accident. Having been unsuccessful in her claim, Ms Dominguez brought an appeal on a point of law to the Cour de cassation (French Court of Cassation). This Court asks the Court of Justice whether the French rules, which make entitlement to paid annual leave conditional on an employee having worked a minimum of 10 days (or, up until February 2008, one month) for the same employer during the reference period (normally one year) are compatible with the 2003/88 Working Time Directive.

Held: The Court held that the directive must be interpreted as pre-cluding a national provision which makes entitlement to paid annual leave conditional on a minimum period of 10 days' (or one month's) actual work during the reference period. Moreover, the Court confirms that the directive does not make any distinction between workers who are absent from work on sick leave during the reference period and those who have in fact worked in the course of that period. It follows that, with regard to workers on sick leave which has been duly granted, the right to paid annual leave conferred by that directive on all workers cannot therefore be made subject by a Member State to a condition that the worker has actually worked during the reference period. Secondly, the Court states that, when applying domestic law, national courts are bound to interpret it, so far as possible, in the light of the wording and the purpose of the directive.

Commentary: This case illustrates the rights that an individual has in order to enforce an EU right against the government of a Member State. In this judgment the developments of indirect effect and state liability are clearly highlighted as the Court states that as she has been unsuccessful in seeking to enforce the Directive against her employer she can bring an action for damages against the French government.

CHECKPOINT

The conditions for imposing state liability are:

1. The rule of Union law infringed must be intended to confer rights on individuals;
2. the breach must be sufficiently serious to justify imposing state liability; and
3. there must be a causal link between the breach of the obligation imposed on the state and the damage actually suffered by the applicant.

These three conditions are a development of those stated in *Francovich*. The decisive test for finding that a breach of community law was sufficiently serious was whether the member state or the Community institution had manifestly and gravely disregarded the limits on its discretion (see Lord Bingham's judgment in *R. v Secretary of State for the Home Department, Ex p. Gallagher* [1996] 2 C.M.L.R. 951). The case of C-453/99 *Courage Ltd v Crehan* illustrates how the Francovich principle has developed. Here an individual sought to bring an action against another individual as they had suffered damage as a result of a breach of EU competition law. The CJEU confirmed that as no national remedy was available an action may be brought under the

Francovich principle against a Member State but also against private individuals or bodies that caused the damage through a breach of Union law.

You should now know and understand:

☐ the relationship between Union and national law

☐ the supremacy of EU law

☐ the difference between a monist and a dualist system of law

☐ the meaning of "direct effect" and the conditions required to enforce it

☐ direct effect of Treaty articles

☐ direct effect of Regulations, Directives and Decisions

☐ the difference between vertical and horizontal direct effect

☐ the development and application of indirect effect

☐ the development and application of the principle of State liability

☐ the conditions required for State liability to be imposed

SUMMARY OF KEY CASES

Case	Court	Key Principle
C-101/87 Bork International v Forening af Arbejdsledere I Danmark	CJEU	Courts can apply the interpretation of EU Directive from CJEU judgments.
C-46/93 Brasserie du Pecheur SA v Germany	CJEU	Developed the principles in Francovich case to apply to liability and thus widened the interpretation of 'State'.
Conseil d'Etat in Minister of the Interior v Cohn-Bendit [1980] 1 C.M.L.R. 543.	Conseil d'Etat	Conseil d'Etat refused to follow Van Duyn v Home Office to allow claimant to invoke direct effect of Directive.
C-6/64 Costa v ENEL	CJEU	Court identified that the EU was a 'new legal order' which became an integral part of the law of the Member States.

C-453/99 Courage Ltd v Crehan	CJEU	An individual can rely upon a breach of art.101(1) TFEU before a national court.
C-148/78 Criminal proceedings against Tullio Ratti	CJEU	Ratti could rely on a Directive that had direct effect but which the Member State had failed to implement.
C-168/95 Criminal proceedings against Luciano Arcaro).	CJEU	No obligation could be impose on an individual by an unimplemented Directive.
C-43/75 Defrenne v Sabena (No.2)	CJEU	The Court said that 'equal pay for equal work' sufficiently clear to create direct effect.
C-282/10 Dominguez v Centre informatique du Centre Ouest Atlantique, Préfet de région Centre	CJEU	When applying domestic law, national courts are bound to interpret it, so far as possible, in the light of the wording and the purpose of the directive.
C-208/90 Emmott v Minister for Social Welfare	CJEU	Until a Directive has been properly implemented the Member State cannot rely upon national time limits to deny a claimant.
Equal Opportunities Commission v Secretary of State for Employment	House of Lords (now the Supreme Court)	Qualifying periods of employment in the UK's Employment Protection (Consolidation) Act 1978 were contrary to EU law—they differentiated unfairly between part-time and full-time employees.
C-57/67 Firma Alfons Lut- ticke GmbH v Hauptzollamt	CJEU	Discriminatory excise duties are prohibited by EU law.
C-91/92 Faccini Dori v Recreb Srl (1995)	CJEU	Advocate General proposed that the claimant should be able to use direct effect of a Directive against a private company. CJEU refused to follow this and applied Marshall judgment so no direct effect.

C-9/70 Franz Grad v Finanzamt Traunstein	CJEU	A Decision could have direct effect if conditions are satisfied.
C-6 & 90/90 Francovich v Italian State	CJEU	CJEU extended the principle of State liability.
Litster v Forth Dry Dock & Engineering Co Ltd [1990] 1 A.C.	House of Lords (now the Supreme Court)	HL interpreted the English legislation to give full effect to the Directive.
C-144/04Mangold v Helm	CJEU	The CJEU enforced Directive 2000/78, which was not yet transposed into national law by using the general principle of non-discrimination.
C-271/91 Marshall v Southampton and South West Hampshire AHA	CJEU	National measures which cap compensation at very low levels are illegal.
C-106/89 Marleasing SA v La Comercial Internacional de Ali-mentacion SA,	CJEU	This case expanded indirect effect by requiring all national legislation to be interpreted in the light of EU law and increased the national courts'interpretive duties.
C-80/86 Officer van Justitie v Koplinghuis Nijmegen	CJEU	The EU principle of legal certainty and non-retroactivity limited the application of the von Colson principle in criminal prosecutions.
C-93/71 Leonesio v Ministero dell'agricoltura e foreste	CJEU	Regulations are capable of having direct effect.
C-43/71 Politi v Ministry for Finance of the Italian Republic	CJEU	The important question is whether it fulfils a 'judicial function' and not what the court is called.
C-213/89 R. v Secretary of State for Transport, Ex p. Factortame Ltd. (No 2)	CJEU	This case presents a major statement by the CJEU on the supremacy of EU law over national law.

C-48/93 R. v Secretary of State for Transport, Ex p. Factortame Ltd	CJEU	Case heard together with C-46/93 Brasserie du Pecheur SA v Germany—see above.
C-92/78 Simmenthal v Commission	CJEU	It is not the form of the EU act which is decisive but its substance so that a 'regulation' may be a 'decision' and not of general application.
C-8/81 Ursula Becker v Finanzamt Munster-Innenstadt	CJEU	Claimant could rely upon a Directive that had not been implemented by the German government.
C-14/83 Von Colson and Kamann v Land Nordrhein-Westfalen and C- 79/83 Harz v Deutsche Tradax GmbH	CJEU	CJEU introduced principle of indirect effect.
C-26/62 Van Gend en Loos v Nederlanse Tariefcommissie	CJEU	CJEU stated that the '[Union] constitutes a new legal order in international law, for whose benefits the States have limited their sovereign rights, albeit within limited fields'.
Webb v EMO Air Cargo (UK) Ltd	House of Lords (now the Supreme Court)	The obligation to interpret national legislation in accordance with EU law applies only so far as such an interpretation is possible.
C-41/74 Yvonne Van Duyn v Home Office	CJEU	The Court held that Directives can be directly effective if they satisfy the criteria in Van Gend en Loos.

QUESTION AND ANSWER

QUESTION

Critically review the requirements for direct effect of EU law.

ADVICE AND THE ANSWER

Introduction—the principle of direct effect has been developed by the CJEU in its early judgments in the 1960s such as *Costa v ENEL* and *Van Gend en Loos v Nederlanse Tariefcommissie*. The benefit this provides to the individual is that they can use the principle to enforce Community rights in their national courts but within the test set by the Court.

The requirements are that the provision must be clear and unambiguous, it must be unconditional and its operation must not be dependent on further action being taken by Union or national authorities.

The initial application of the principle was to Treaty provisions (*Van Gend en Loos*) but it has also been applied to Regulations (*Politi v Ministry for Finance of the Italian Republic*) and Decisions (*Franz Grad v Finanzamt Traunstein*).

The main issue has been whether the test can be applied to Directives given the definition of these measures under art.288 **TFEU**. In the case of *Van Duyn v Home Office* it was decided that Directives could have direct effect if the test is satisfied and there is a situation of "vertical direct effect" involving an emanation of the State. If there was no relationship with the State, for example where the employer was a private company, then the individual could not enforce the Community right.

This failure to use direct effect has led the court to introduce indirect effect but many see this as an artificial solution which could be removed if the distinction between vertical and horizontal direct effect was removed. This is something the CJEU has been reluctant to do.

EU AND NATIONAL LAW

Preliminary References

5

INTRODUCTION

In English law it is not unknown for senior judges to provide guidance by answering specific questions, as demonstrated by the "appeal by case stated" procedure. However the EU system of preliminary references is much more important and has had a much greater impact on our law. The intention was to provide a procedure that would allow for consistency of interpretation and application of EU law in the Member States but it has been used effectively by the CJEU to create principles like supremacy and direct effect. In this way the influence of European law and the impact on the individual has been extended.

Under the system of preliminary references a court in any Member State may make a reference to the CJEU in order to ascertain its view with regard to the interpretation or validity. The case in the Member States is suspended while the question(s) are despatched for consideration by the CJEU. When the Court has given its judgment the answers are sent back to the national courts which, having had the Union law clarified for them, apply it to the case before them in the normal way. The period that it takes for this process to take place is around 18 months, although every effort is made by the CJEU to reduce this timescale.

Objectives of preliminary references

As was shown in Ch.4 above, p.43 the principle was established whereby Union law must override national law in the event of a conflict. To do otherwise would allow a Member State to avoid the application of Union law which they considered disadvantageous by the simple expedient of passing conflicting legislation for their national courts to apply. As Union law does have this superiority over national law it is important that such law should have the same meaning and effect in all Member States. This requires that there should be a single court, the CJEU, whose jurisdiction extends over the whole European Union. Also, if Union law is under certain circumstances to be directly effective, the CJEU must have the final say with regard to its validity and interpretation. Thus the objectives of the preliminary reference procedure under art.267 TFEU is to provide for a definitive judgment regarding the interpretation and validity of Union law.

Matters for referral under article 267 TFEU

There are two parts to art.267(1) TFEU and both are important as they state that the EU Courts have the ability to give preliminary rulings on:

(a) the interpretation of the Treaty; and

(b) the validity and interpretation of acts of the institutions, bodies, offices or agencies of the Union.

There is an obvious distinction in that there is only the possibility of seeking interpretation of the Treaty as its validity cannot be challenged. This is what one would expect when the Treaty is seen as the primary source of Union or Community law. The "acts of the institutions" refers to the European Parliament, Council and Commission making legally binding acts defined in art.288 TFEU such as Regulations and Directives.

Direct effect and art.267 TFEU references   There are two important points to make which show that the list above is not exhaustive. First, as was shown in the last chapter, the principle of direct effect has had an important influence on the development of Union law. The CJEU has used the procedure for preliminary rulings to look at the effectiveness of EU provisions, as well as the supremacy of EU law. The majority of the most important cases on Union law have been brought before the Court by the art.267 TFEU procedure. Although the Court would argue that it is merely exercising its authority as interpreter of Union law, it is in reality going much further than what would normally be regarded as interpretation. This is sometimes referred to as the judicial activism of the CJEU, such as where the Court effectively extends the competences of the Union beyond the bounds set by the Treaties. In the recent case of C-34/09 *Gerardo Ruiz Zambrano v Office national de l'emploi (ONEM)*, the Court has significantly extended the scope of European Citizenship (see Ch.12 below).

The result is that there are really three issues which may be referred to the Court for a ruling: interpretation, effect and, for certain provisions, validity. Questions of fact and of national law may not be referred, nor may the Court rule on the application of the law to the particular facts of the case. However, the boundary between interpretation and application is sometime uncertain, and although the CJEU may cross it the national court receiving the ruling can decide for itself.

The second point is that wherever possible the Court has taken a liberal view with regard to the "acts" of the institutions it is called upon to consider. It is not restricted to art.288 TFEU. For example, although agreements with non-Member States are clearly not part of the Treaty they are negotiated by the Commission and concluded by the Council under procedures and powers to be found in art.218 TFEU of the Treaty. Thus in Case 181/73 *R & V*

Haegeman v Belgium the Court seized upon this ground for regarding the Association Agreement between the Community and Greece as a Community act and therefore covered by art.267(1)(b) TFEU. Having done this the Court then went on to interpret the Agreement itself! The view of the Court is that since such international agreements are part of EU law and binding on the Member States, it is clearly desirable that they should receive uniform interpretation throughout the Union. Obviously the ruling of the Court is not binding on the other party, i.e. Greece in the *Haegeman* case as they were not members of the Union at that time.

General principles of EU law may not form the subject matter of a reference as they are neither part of the Treaty nor are they Union or Community acts. However, as was illustrated above, the art.267 TFEU procedure has been used with regard to them by the simple expedient of using a suitable Treaty provision or Community act to provide a peg on which to hang the general principle. The latter can then be interpreted in the course of the reference. Which courts are covered by art.267 TFEU?

Article 267(2) and 267(3) TFEU both refer to courts and tribunals. There are two requirements that these must fulfil. First, the body requesting the reference must be a court or tribunal and, second, they must be of a Member State. This second requirement is straightforward but the first has produced some clear statements from the Court.

Court or tribunal? For the CJEU it does not matter what the body is called or whether it is recognised as a court or tribunal under national law. The key question of the Court is whether it performs a judicial function. What constitutes a "judicial function" is not always easy to clarify but, generally, a body is regarded as judicial if it has power to give binding determinations of the legal rights and obligations of individuals. In Case 61/65 *Vaassen v Beamtenfonds Mijnbedrij* a reference was made by an "arbitration tribunal", which settled disputes regarding the pension fund for the Dutch mining industry. The fund had been set up privately with representatives of both employers and employees and was approved by the ministers responsible for both the mines and social security. Members of the tribunal were appointed by the minister and any pension dispute had to go before it and be subject to its adversary procedure. The Court of Justice concluded that this tribunal came within art.267 TFEU because it was a judicial body representing the power of the State and settling as a matter of law disputes concerning the application of the pension scheme. In contrast, the CJEU refused to give a ruling in Case 138/80 *Borker, Re* on a reference from the Paris Chambre des Avocats on the ground that it was not exercising a judicial function. In Cases 69/96–79/96 *Garofalo v Ministera della Sanita* the CJEU specified a number of factors to be taken into account in order to determine whether a body is a "court or tribunal". The conclusion from this is that all administrative tribunals established in the UK by statute would be recognised as having a right under art.267 TFEU to make a reference. However, if they were merely domestic tribunals the CJEU would have to decide whether the element of acting for the state, the adversarial procedure and possible recourse to the national courts were -sufficient for it to be within the art.267 TFEU procedure.

Preliminary references and national law

Where a court or tribunal has a right to make a reference under art.267 TFEU, it cannot be deprived of that right by national law. The Court stated this rule in the *Rheinmuhlen* cases which were heard in the German Tax Courts. The lower court hearing the case wished to make a reference to the CJEU as a number of questions had been raised which required interpretation. This was despite a ruling having been given to it by the higher Federal Tax Court. In the end both German courts made a reference. The Federal Tax Court asked whether art.267 TFEU gives lower courts an unfettered right to refer, or whether it is subject to national provisions under which lower courts are bound by the judgments of superior courts. The response of the CJEU was unequivocal. The power of a lower court to make a reference cannot be abrogated by a provision of national law. Lower courts must be free to make a reference if it considers that the superior court's ruling could lead it to give judgment contrary to Community law (see Chadwick L.J. in *Trent Taverns Ltd v Sykes* [1999] EU.L.R. 492).

The practical situation is that national law cannot take away the right given by art.267(2) TFEU. In *R. v Plymouth Justices, Ex p. Rogers* [1982] Q.B. 863, Lord Lane C.J. stated that magistrates had the jurisdiction to make a reference but that they should consider whether a higher court might be in a better position to assess the need for a reference and to formulate the questions to be sent to the Court. A counter argument has been put in that if a reference seems likely to be made at some stage in the proceedings, time may actually be saved if this is done as soon as possible, for an appeal within the domestic system may thereby be obviated.

Article 267(2) TFEU

The word "may" appears in this article, giving those courts and tribunals concerned a discretion as to whether or not to make a reference to the CJEU. There are two requisites which have to be fulfilled before art.267(2) TFEU comes into operation.

1. An appropriate question of EU law must be raised before the court. In fact the "question" can be raised by either the parties to the action or the court itself, as is allowed for under the procedural rules in England (Civil Procedure Rules (CPR) Pt 68).

2. A decision on that question must be necessary to enable the court to give judgment. It should be noted that it is not the reference which is necessary but a decision on the question. The Treaty makes it clear that this is for the national court to decide and the CJEU will not question the necessity of the decision or whether Community law is even applicable to the case. Lord Denning in *Bulmer v Bollinger* [1974] 3 W.L.R 202 said that "necessary" meant that the outcome of the case must be dependent on the decision. "If the Community [EU] point is decided one way, judgment for one party must be the result; if it decided in another way, judgment must be given for the other party". This is perhaps too restrictive an interpretation. A better suggestion is that "necessary" should be interpreted to mean that the point could be decisive. To assist in this process it is better if the facts of the case are fully ascertained before a reference is made. This will help because it may result in the national court deciding that the case can be settled on a point of national law and a reference would not be required. However, it should be remembered that under Civil Procedure Rules (CPR) Part 68 a reference may be made at any stage in the proceedings. In Case 157/92 *Pretore di Genova v Banchero* the CJEU said that the national court must define the factual and legal framework in which the questions arise before making a preliminary reference.

Previous judgments of the CJEU to preliminary references

It may be that the question for interpretation or validity specified in art.267(1) TFEU has already come before the Court and it has provided an answer. In such circumstances the point may be regarded as settled and the authority of the previous ruling would remove the need to make a reference. However, it should be remembered that the CJEU does not have the same judicial tradition towards precedent as English courts, and that if the national court wishes to exercise the right under art.267 TFEU it cannot be fettered.

Article 267(3) TFEU

This article appears to lay down an obligation to make a reference where the court or tribunal of a Member State is one "against whose decision there is no judicial remedy under national law". What courts are included? There are two propositions, an Abstract Theory and a Concrete Theory.

The literal reading of art.267(3) TFEU would seem to favour the Abstract Theory. Certainly Lord Denning was of the opinion in *Bulmer v Bollinger* that only the House of Lords (now the Supreme Court) came with the scope of this article. However, the CJEU appears to favour the Concrete Theory when it suggests that art.267(3) TFEU refers to the highest court in the case rather than the highest court in the Member State (*Costa v ENEL*). The case of *Chiron*

Corp v Murex Diagnostics [1994] F.S.R. 202 discussed these issues in relation to the Court of Appeal and the then House of Lords (now the Supreme Court).

CHECKPOINT

Abstract theory

Only those courts whose decisions are never subject to appeal are within the scope of this provision. For example, in the UK the Supreme Court would obviously be the only court in this category.

Concrete theory

The important question is whether the court's decision in the case in question is subject to appeal. An example of this would be the case of *Costa v ENEL*, where the sum involved in the case meant that there could be no appeal from the lower court within the Italian court system.

Obligation to refer

As early as Case 28/62 *Da Costa en Schaake v Netherlands Inland Revenue Administration* the CJEU had stated that if the Court had already pronounced on a question of interpretation it might deprive the obligation to refer of its purpose and empty it of its substance. The important CJEU judgment in Case 283/81 *CILFIT v Ministry of Health* put the obligation on art.267(3) TFEU courts to make a reference in a clearer position. In this case the Court said that the obligation to refer was based on co-operation between the national courts and the European Court. The purpose of this co-operation was to prevent divergences in judicial decisions on question of EU law, i.e. uniformity. It may be that the correct application of Union law was so obvious that there was no scope for reasonable doubt about the answers to any questions raised. This reflects the principle of *acte clair*.

Acte Clair

This principle has its origins in French law, where the ordinary courts were required to request a ruling from the Ministry of Foreign Affairs on a question of treaty interpretation unless the point was regarded as clear. Thus, in relation to preliminary references under art.267(3) TFEU, the courts might consider that the state of EU law is sufficiently clear to be applied without the need for a reference to be made. This would assist in the workload of the CJEU and perhaps is overdue in that the national courts affected by the principle are those which contain experienced and well qualified judges. However, the Court did give a warning to those who wished to apply the principle of *acte clair*. They should remember that although the matter may be obvious to them, is it equally obvious to the courts in other Member States and the CJEU itself? The Court specifically mentioned three particular difficulties:

1. Union or Community legislation is drafted in several languages and that the different language versions are all equally authentic. Any interpretation therefore involves the comparison of different language versions.

2. EU law uses terminology which is peculiar to itself and some legal concepts do not necessarily have the same meaning in Union law or in the various Member States.

3. Every provision of EU law must be placed in its context and interpreted in the light of provisions of Union law as a whole (see Interpretation above, p.38).

KEY CASE

CASE 283/81 CILFIT V MINISTRY OF HEALTH

Facts: This case involved a number of textile firms in Italy (CILFIT) challenging an EU levy on wool imported from outside the Union, as required by an EU Regulation dealing with animal products. The Italian Ministry of Health argued that there was no need to make a preliminary reference to the CJEU as it was obvious that wool was an animal product. The Italian court decided to make a reference anyway and the judgment of the CJEU has proved to be of great importance.

Held: The Court said that art.234(3) **EC** (now art.267(3) **TFEU**) does place an obligation to refer on the court unless it was established (a) that the question raised is irrelevant or (b) has already been interpreted or (c) that the correct application of Community law is so obvious as to leave no scope for any reasonable doubt. art.267(3) **TFEU** as a strict one subject to derogations such as where the Court had already pronounced on the subject. CILFIT shows the CJEU accepting the principle of *acte clair*.

However, the national court still remains entirely at liberty to make a reference if it wishes. In the UK the Supreme Court has adopted the approach recommended by the CJEU in *CILFIT*.

Guidelines and procedures used in the English courts

As was stated above the national courts cannot be fettered by national rules when it comes to exercising their rights to make a preliminary reference. Having accepted this principle a number of guidelines have been given to help the court or tribunal decide whether or when to make a reference.

BULMER V BOLLINGER [1974]

Facts: Bulmer's are producers of cider in England who market some of their products as 'champagne cider' and 'champagne perry'. Bollinger's are French producers of 'champagne' who objected to the use of their name by Bulmer as it misled consumers to think that their products resembled 'champagne'. The parties suggested that a reference should be made to the CJEU so that the Regulation concerning the labelling of wine could be interpreted.

Held: The appeal by Bulmer's was refused and no reference would be made to the European Court of Justice.

Commentary: The importance of this case is that Lord Denning in *Bulmer v Bollinger* [1974] was the first senior judge to provide some guidance for lower courts with regard to how art.177 EC (now art.267 **TFEU**). The system of requesting a preliminary ruling was new to English law as the UK only joined the EU in 1973. He said that the following facts should be taken into account:

(a) the facts should be decided first, so that the question of whether it was "necessary" could be settled;

(b) the reference to Luxembourg will cause delay and therefore add to the costs of the parties, so the lower court should deal with the case and leave it to an appeal court to decide whether or not to make a reference;

(c) the difficulty or importance of the question;

(d) the wishes of the parties should be taken into account, although it was the court's decision whether to make a reference or not; and

(e) the need to avoid overloading the CJEU.

These guidelines are still used by the English Courts, although other judges have clarified them. See MacPherson J. in *R. v HM Treasury, Ex p. Daily Mail & General Trust Plc* [1989] 1 All E.R. 328, Kerr L.J. in *R. v The Pharmaceutical Society of Great Britain, Ex p. the Association of Pharmaceutical Importers* [1987] 3 C.M.L.R. 951 and Bingham M.R. in *The Stock Exchange* case (1993).

Civil Procedure Rules (CPR) Part 68

Once a court or tribunal has decided to make a reference the procedure for it to be made in England is provided by the Civil Procedure Rules Pt 68. Although this rule applies specifically to the High Court and the Court of Appeal similar provisions are applicable in the other courts for which no special provision has been made. The court frames the questions it wishes answered and the Senior Master sends a copy to the Registrar of the European Court. There is sometimes a delay where the reference is being made by the High Court, to allow for any appeal against the reference to be made to the Court of Appeal. While a reply is awaited from the CJEU the proceedings in the national court are stayed.

Effects of a preliminary ruling

The national court or tribunal, which made the reference, may actually decide the case on other grounds, but if it does apply Union law it is bound by the ruling of the CJEU. As far as other courts are concerned they may accept the interpretation in the ruling which makes it unnecessary for them to make their own reference on the same point of Union law, but they can still make a separate reference if they wish. In the case of C-487/07 *L'Oreal SA & Others v Bellure NV & Others* a trade mark was involved in a dispute which came before the Court of Appeal (Civil Division). The judge, Jacob L.J. made a reference under art.267 TFEU but was of the opposite view to that of the CJEU when he received their judgment. He said that "My duty as a national judge is to follow EU law interpreted by the CJEU ... As I have said I do not agree with or welcome this conclusion—it amounts to a pointless monopoly. But my duty is to apply it".

Refusal of a preliminary reference

The CJEU recognises that the preliminary reference procedure has an important contribution to make towards the co-operation it seeks to develop with national courts. It is very rare for the CJEU to refuse a reference if the court or tribunal making it comes within art.267 TFEU. However, in the *Foglia v Novello* cases (Cases 104/79 and 244/80 respectively) the Court refused a reference because it felt that there was an absence of any real legal dispute between the parties. It was felt that this case would herald a restrictive approach by the CJEU but this has not happened. In Case 150/88 *Parfumerie-Fabrik v Provide* the CJEU confirmed that it would not lightly infer an absence of a genuine dispute between the parties. In Case 89/91 *Meilicke v ADV/ ORGA FA Meyer* the Court ruled that "the spirit of cooperation which must prevail in preliminary ruling proceedings requires the national court to have regard to the function entrusted to the Court of Justice, which is to contribute to the administration of justice in member states and not give opinions on general or hypothetical questions". In the recent judgement in Case 318/00 *Bacardi- Martini v Newcastle United FC* the CJEU said that it had to apply special vigilance when a reference came in from one Member State seeking to question the compatibility of legislation in another Member State with EU law. In that case the Court refused to deal with the reference about TV advertising of alcohol under French law.

Preliminary rulings on validity

In Case 314/85 *Foto-Frost v Hauptzollamt Lubeck Ost* the CJEU held that national courts were entitled to find that acts adopted by the institutions of the Union were valid, but they had no power in normal proceedings to declare such acts invalid. This is to stop them placing in jeopardy the unity of the Community or Union legal order and would detract from the fundamental requirement of legal certainty. The only exception to this would possibly be in interlocutory proceedings. If a national court suspects that an act may be invalid a reference must be made.

REVISION CHECKLIST

You should now know and understand:

- [ ] objectives of the system of preliminary references
- [ ] what can be the subject of a reference under art.267(1) TFEU
- [ ] the development of the principle of Direct Effect and the system of preliminary references
- [ ] the definitions used to determine whether the reference is from a "court or tribunal"
- [ ] the relationship between preliminary references and national law
- [ ] the discretion under art.234(2) EC compared with the "duty" under art.267(3) TFEU
- [ ] the principle of *acte clair*
- [ ] the guidelines produced to assist judges when deciding to make a reference
- [ ] the effects of a preliminary ruling
- [ ] the refusal of a preliminary reference
- [ ] the situation where the preliminary rulings is about validity

SUMMARY OF KEY CASES

Case	Court	Key Principle
C-318/00 Bacardi-Martini v Newcastle United FC	CJEU	Preliminary reference rejected because it was questioning the compatibility with EU law of law of another Member State.

C-138/80 Borker, Re	CJEU	Refused a preliminary reference because the body was not 'exercising a judicial function'.
Bulmer v Bollinger	Court of Appeal (Civil Division)	Lord Denning said that 'necessary' for the purposes of a preliminary ruling meant that the outcome must be dependent on the decision.
C-283/81 CILFIT v Ministry of Health	CJEU	The CJEU provided guidance on the application of acte clair for art.267(3) TFEU courts.
C-28/62 Da Costa en Schaake v Netherlands Inland Revenue Administration	CJEU	A preliminary reference might be not be necessary where CJEU has already pronounced on a question of interpretation.
C-104/79 & 244/79 Foglia v Novello cases	CJEU	The CJEU will not answer hypothetical questions.
C-314/85 Foto-Frost v Hauptzollamt Lubeck Ost	CJEU	Member States' courts can find an EU measure valid but have no powers to declare such acts invalid.
C-69/96–79/96 Garofalo v Ministera della Sanita	CJEU	All UK administrative tribunals established by statute would be recognised as having right under art.267 TFEU to make a reference.
C-34/09 Gerardo Ruiz Zambrano v. Office national de l'emploi (ONEM),	CJEU	Member State are precluded from refusing a third country national with dependent children who are European Union citizens a right of residence in the Member State and from refusing to grant a work permit to that third country national.
C-487/07 L'Oreal SA & Others v Bellure NV & Others	CJEU	Duty of national judge is to follow EU law as interpreted by the CJEU.

C-89/91 Meilicke v ADV/ORGA FA Meyer	CJEU	The preliminary reference procedure should be seen as a partnership between the national courts and CJEU.
C-150/88 Parfumerie-Fabrik v Provide	CJEU	The CJEU would not lightly infer an absence of a genuine dispute between the parties when receiving a request for a preliminary reference.
C-157/92 Pretore di Genova v Banchero	CJEU	National court must define factual and legal framework when making a reference.
C-181/73 R & V Haegeman v Belgium	CJEU	CJEU has given a wide definition of 'Union acts' to include international agreements.
R. v Plymouth Justices, Ex p. Rogers [1982] Q.B. 863, Lord Lane C.J.	CJEU	Lower courts cannot be deprived of the right to make a request for a preliminary ruling but guidance is provided.
C-166/73 Rheinmuhlen	CJEU	The power of a lower court cannot be abrogated by a provision of national law.
C-61/65 Vaassen v Beamtenfonds Mijnbedrij	CJEU	The tribunal could use art.267 TFEU because it was fulfilling a judicial function giving judgments that were binding on the parties.

QUESTION AND ANSWER

QUESTION

What guidelines are provided for national judges considering making a preliminary reference under art.267 TFEU?

Introduction—The preliminary reference procedure allows courts or tribunals in Member States to ask the CJEU or the General Court questions on Union law as defined by art.267(1) TFEU. The article itself provides some guidance in art.234(1) and (2) TFEU in relation to those courts that may or shall make a reference but case law has also provided some guidance.

A court in a Member State cannot be stopped from making a reference (*Rheinmuhlen* cases) but guidance is permitted. For courts which are not the final court in the case Denning has provided some guidance in *Bulmer v Bollinger* [1974], he was the first senior judge to provide some guidance for lower courts. He said that the following should be taken into account:

(a) the facts should be decided first, so that the question of whether it was "necessary" could be settled;

(b) the reference to Luxembourg will cause delay and therefore add to the costs of the parties, so the lower court should deal with the case and leave it to an appeal court to decide whether or not to make a reference;

(c) the difficulty or importance of the question;

(d) the wishes of the parties should be taken into account, although it was the court's decision whether to make a reference or not, and

(e) the need to avoid overloading the CJEU.

These guidelines have been expanded by subsequent senior judges including Lord Bingham in the *Stock Exchange* case (1993).

With regard to those courts which come within art.267(3) TFEU such as the Supreme Court, the CJEU itself has provided some guidelines when it accepted the principle of acte clair for Union law. In the case of (C283/81) *CILTFIT v Ministry of Health* the CJEU raised some circumstances where it might be better for a court to make a reference rather than to decide the law themselves.

Judicial Remedies and Review

....

6

INTRODUCTION

Although the indirect action associated with a request for a preliminary reference is important, there are a number of direct actions specified in the Treaties. These actions cover a range of actions that can be brought by the European Commission, a Member State or other specified person but they are restrictively interpreted by the CJEU. This means that they are not used as much as perhaps the authors of the Treaties envisaged. This chapter reviews these types of actions and the interpretation given to them by the CJEU.

....

ENFORCEMENT ACTIONS BY THE EUROPEAN COMMISSION

In Case 6/64 *Costa v ENEL* the Court of Justice stressed the point that the Community was a new legal order which required Community law to be obeyed. If this did not happen the "legal basis of the Union itself would be called into question". There needs to be, therefore, a mechanism for forcing the Member States to fulfil their obligations under the Treaty. As was stated in Ch.3 above, p., the European Commission have been given the general duty under art.17 TEU to "ensure that the provisions of this Treaty and the measures taken by the institutions pursuant thereto are applied". The Commission has been given this power under art.258 TFEU. The art.258 TFEU procedure can be initiated whenever the Commission considers that a Member State has failed to fulfil an obligation under the Treaty. This would include breach of administrative acts, general principles of Union law or international agreements. The breach may take the form of either an act or an omission such as the non-implementation of EC law or the retention of national laws which conflict with EC law. One of the problems for the Commission is that they receive many complaints that Member States are failing to fulfil their obligations. They come from individuals, companies, trade unions, pressure groups, MEPs and even from other governments. Member States have a legal duty to co-operate with the Commission investigations into alleged breaches by them (Case 45/93 *Commission v Spain*).

There are two stages to the procedure; an administrative stage and a judicial stage. The administrative stage is where the Director-General responsible for the policy of the Union will write to the Member State informing it that the Commission has formed the view that there is a breach of an obligation under the Treaty. Obviously there has been some investigation by the Director-General's office before this happens. The Member State then has an opportunity to answer the allegations or rectify the position. This is a very delicate stage because no government likes to be considered in breach of a treaty obligation. If, after receiving a reply from the Member State, the Commission considers that the Member State has been in breach it may deliver a reasoned opinion.

Reasoned opinion

The reasoned opinion is a very important document because it will form the basis of the legal proceedings under art.258 TFEU if the Commission decides to go on to that stage. At this stage the reasoned opinion is considered confidential and is not legally binding and cannot be challenged (Case 4/69 *Alfons Lutticke GmbH v E.C. Commission No.1*). It has two purposes:

1. It must set out the reasons of facts and law for which the Commission considers that the Member State concerned has failed to fulfil its obligations; and
2. It must inform the State of the measures which the Commission considers necessary to bring the failure to an end.

The Treaty does not specify the time-scale in which this must take place, but a reasonable time must be given by the Commission. The delivery of the reasoned opinion marks the end of the administrative stage.

The Commission has discretion as to whether to take the procedure on to the next stage. Advocate-General Roemer in Case 26/69 *Commission v France* suggested a number of situations in which the Commission might be justified in not initiating the enforcement procedure. These included the possibility that an amicable settlement could be achieved if formal proceedings were delayed, or where the effects of the violation were only minor, or where there is a possibility that the Union provision in question might be altered in the near future. Other situations that have been put forward are where the breach is the isolated act of an official or where action might inflame a politically sensitive situation. It is interesting to note that no action has been brought against the violation of Union law by national courts, even in situations like the *Cohn-Bendit* judgment in 1978. This is perhaps due to the fear that such an action might be seen as undermining the independence of the judiciary (see *Syndicat General de Fabricants de Semoules de France* [1970] C.M.L.R 395). However in Case 224/01 *Kobler v Austria*, the Austrian

Administrative court refused to make a preliminary reference and declared that the calculation of a university professor's pay was compatible with Union law. In its judgement the CJEU said that a breach of Union law by a national court may make the state liable in damages if the breach was "manifest and sufficiently serious". This would seem to open the possibility of an enforcement action if the breach persisted.

KEY CASE

CASE 224/01 KOBLER V AUSTRIA

Facts: Köbler had been employed since March 1, 1986 as an ordinary university professor in Innsbruck (Austria). In 1996 he applied for the special length-of-service increment for university professors. The grant of that benefit is dependent under Austrian law on the completion of 15 years' service solely in Austrian universities. Köbler had completed the requisite length of service if the duration of his service in universities of other Member States were taken into consideration. When this was refused Köbler brought proceedings before the Austrian Supreme Administrative Court, arguing that such a requirement constituted indirect discrimination contrary to EU law. On that point the Supreme Administrative Court of last instance in Austria made a reference to the Court of Justice of the European Union but withdrew the application when the CJEU gave a judgment in a similar case (Case C-15/96 *Schöning-Kougebetopoulou*). The Austrian court then went on to dismiss Köbler's action on the ground that the special length-of-service increment was a loyalty bonus which justified derogation from the provisions on freedom of movement for workers. Köbler brought an action for damages before the Civil Court in Vienna against the Republic of Austria on the ground that the judgment of the Administrative Court was contrary to EU law. This court then made a reference to the CJEU.

Held: The system of the EU Treaty requires the Member States to afford reparation of damage caused to individuals as a result of breaches of Union law for which they are responsible, whichever is the authority of the Member State responsible for the damage. The Court then said that the three conditions identified in the *Francovich* case and refined in *Brasserie du Pêcheur* and *Factortame* cases (see above). Having applied the conditions the Court came to the conclusion that Austrian Supreme Administrative Court did not commit a manifest and thus sufficiently serious breach of Community law; consequently, the Austrian State does not incur liability for it.

> **Commentary:** This case was a further development in the extension of Member State liability for damages under art.340(2) **TFEU**. It was important as it introduced an obligation on Member States to make good any damage caused to individuals where there has been an infringement of EU law attributable to national courts of last instance adjudicating on a case before them. The protection of rights given to individuals by EU law would be weakened if such individuals could not obtain damages where their EU rights had been infringed.

Interim measures

An application for interim relief can be made to the CJEU at any time once the administrative stage of the art.258 TFEU procedure has been completed. Article 279 TFEU: "The Court of Justice may in any cases brought before it prescribe any necessary interim measures". In such situations the European Commission must show that a prima facie case is made out and that the urgency of the situation requires action by the Court.

Judicial stage

If the Member State has not rectified its breach and the time period has elapsed, the Commission may bring the matter before the CJEU. This would indicate that the Commission has discretion at this stage. However, the duty under art.17 TEU mentioned above must be remembered. The duty requires the Commission to take appropriate action to ensure that the breach is rectified. Every attempt will be made to reach an amicable settlement.

The Court will consider whether the violation specified in the reasoned opinion has taken place. The Commission cannot raise new violations at the judicial stage. However, the Commission can continue with the action even if the Member State has terminated its infringement during the judicial stage, as happened in Case 7/61 *Commission v Italy (Pork Imports case)*. The Member States put forward many reasons for their failure, some of them quite ingenious. These have included the inability of the national government to get the required legislation through their national parliaments or where trade union pressure prevented the Member State (Case 128/78 *Commission v UK*).

ENFORCEMENT ACTIONS BY A MEMBER STATE

Generally the governments of Member States are prepared to leave breaches of Community obligations by other Member States to the Commission to seek enforcement under art.258 TFEU. It is only in exceptional situations that a

Member State will take on the responsibility itself, but if it does it has the procedure under art.259 TFEU to follow. The applicant Member State has to report the breach to the Commission, which will give the defaulting Member State an opportunity to make representations and carry out its own investigations. If the Commission has not issued a reasoned opinion within three months, the Member State complaining of the breach may bring the matter before the CJEU. It may be that a Member State wants to make a particular political point and for that reason brings the action under art.259 TFEU rather than leaving it to the Commission's procedure (Case 141/78 *France v UK*).

Remedy under article 260 TFEU

Whether the action against a Member State is brought under art.258 or art.259 TFEU, the remedy provided is that of art.260 TFEU. Originally the remedy was only a declaration by the Court that the Member State was in default and that it should take the necessary steps to comply with the judgment of the Court. On some occasions this meant that if the Member State continued with the breach the whole procedure had to be started again. However, this was changed by the Maastricht Treaty on European Union with regards to actions under art.258 TFEU. Now if the Commission considers that the Member State has continued with the breach, it may issue a reasoned opinion after allowing the Member State to make their observations. The reasoned opinion must specify the points where the Member State has not complied with the Court's judgment and give a time limit for compliance to be achieved. If this does not happen the Commission may bring the matter before the Court again, but this time specifying an appropriate lump sum or penalty to be paid by the Member State. If the Court considers that the Member State has not complied with its judgment, it may impose a lump sum or penalty. In January 1997 the Commission agreed a procedure so that it could recommend to the Court the appropriate fine based on a daily fine multiplied by the gravity and the time duration of the breach. The first case brought before the CJEU on the basis of this procedure was Case 387/97 *Commission v Greece*.

KEY CASE

CASE 387/97 COMMISSION V GREECE

In 1987 the Commission received a complaint drawing its attention to uncontrolled waste disposal in the river Kouroupitos, 200 metres from the sea, by several municipalities in the prefecture of Chania (Crete). The waste came from military bases, hospitals and industry in the area. In 1992 the Court of Justice held in a first judgment that Greece had failed to take the necessary measures for toxic and dangerous waste to be disposed of in the area of Chania while ensuring that human health and the environment were protected, as required by two Community directives of 1975 and 1978 which Greece should have applied from 1981.

In 1993 the Commission reminded the Greek authorities of their obligations and at the end of 1995 it decided to initiate a fresh procedure. In 1997 the Commission thus applied to the Court of Justice for an order requiring Greece to pay 24 600 Euros per day of delay from delivery of the new judgment.

Held: The Court upheld the decision of the Commission and found that Greece had not fulfilled its obligations under the Treaties. The Court imposed a periodic penalty payment as the most appropriate means of ensuring that EU law was applied uniformly and effectively and of inducing Greece to comply with its obligations. The suggestions as to the amount by the Commission were a useful point of reference but they were not binding upon the Court. The basic criteria considered by the Court were the duration of the infringement, its degree of seriousness and the ability of the Member State concerned to pay. In applying those criteria, the Court imposed a penalty payment of 20,000 Euros for each day of delay in complying with the 1992 judgment.

Commentary: This possibility of imposing a fine in the form of a lump sum or periodic penalty payment had been introduced by the **Treaty on European Union** (the **Maastricht Treaty**). The basic criteria to be considered are, in principle, the duration of the infringement, its degree of seriousness and the ability of the Member State concerned to pay. In applying those criteria, the Court had regard, in particular, to the effects of the failure to comply on private and public interests and to the urgency of getting the Member State concerned to fulfil its obligations.

In the recent case of Case C-304/02 *Commission v French Republic*, France was ordered to pay a lump sum of 20,000,000 Euros and a penalty payment of 57,761,250 Euros for each six-month period that it continued not to comply with its obligations. Thus the penalty payment is not an alternative to the lump sum payment but can be imposed together if the CJEU considers it appropriate.

There are a number of "mays" in the art.260 TFEU and there was some doubt as to what would happen when the Commission or the Court decided to exercise the new powers given to them. In 1996 the first fines were imposed and the CJEU has noted "that the use of fines has led to a more uniform, complete and simultaneous application of Community law rules in all Member States". However, there continues to be a discretion exercised by the Commission, illustrated by its decision in November 2002 not to take France back to the Court to be fined for the breach associated with the BSE issue surrounding the export of beef from the UK to France.

Action for annulment under article 263 TFEU

The action under art.263 TFEU is a direct challenge upon the validity of a Union act. There are five grounds on which the challenge can be based, the sole purpose of which is to get the act annulled. In any annulment proceedings the CJEU has no other option but to annul or not to annul. It cannot replace the act or amend it. The exception to this is where the Court can declare a regulation void but decide that the particular effects accomplished by it shall remain valid even if only temporarily. This provides time for the Commission or Council to rectify the situation.

Which Acts can be challenged?

The amended art.263 TFEU gives the Court the authority to review the legality of all those acts specified in art.288 TFEU which are intended to be legally binding. Therefore opinions and recommendations are not covered as they are not legally binding. The acts covered include those of the Council, the Commission, the European Parliament and the European Central Bank. However, there is some flexibility.

The most important requirement in any action under this article is that the measure being challenged should be legally binding. Thus in Case 22/70 *EC Commission v EC Council* (the *ERTA* case) the Commission had started actions under art.263 TFEU for the annulment of the Council's discussions resulting in a common position. The Commission disagreed with the procedure adopted by the Council for the negotiations for the European Road Transport Agreement because they felt that this was now a matter for the Community and not the individual Member States. The main point of the case concerned who had competence with regard to external agreements on this policy area. The CJEU held that "it would be inconsistent with the objectives [of the Article] to interpret the conditions under which an action is admissible so restrictively as to limit the availability of this procedure merely to the categories of measures referred to by art.288 TFEU". The Court's judgment in *ERTA* was followed in the more recent Case 294/83 *Les Verts v Parliament* where a French political grouping sought the annulment of two measures adopted by the European Parliament.

Privileged applicants

Under art.263(2) TFEU the European Parliament, the Member States, the Council or the Commission can challenge any legally binding act. They do not have to show any specific locus standi. The European Parliament had made a number of attempts to be accepted by the Court as being within this same category of privileged applicants on the basis that its status had become more important since direct elections. In Case 70/88 *European Parliament v Council* (the Chernobyl case) the CJEU held that Parliament had the right to seek annulment of acts adopted by the Council and the Commission where the purpose of the proceedings was to protect the Parliament's prerogatives. The Treaty of Nice finally included the EP as a fully privileged applicant. Under the provisions of the TEU, the article had been amended to allow for actions by both the Court of Auditors and the ECB for "the purpose of protecting their prerogatives". The case brought by Les Verts against the Parliament mentioned above would now come under art.263(2) TFEU.

Non-privileged applicants

This category of applicant includes all those listed in art.263(4) TFEU, namely any natural or legal person. The ability of these individuals to challenge Community acts are severely restricted, in contrast to the "privileged applicants".

TREATY HIGHLIGHTER

Article 263(4) TFEU Non-privileged applicants may only bring proceedings against three types of act, namely:
(a) a decision addressed to the applicant;
(b) a decision in the form of a regulatory act which is of direct and individual concern to the applicant;
(c) a decision addressed to another person which is of direct and individual concern to the applicant.

This shows that if a decision is addressed to an individual, as would happen, e.g. in competition policy cases, he may challenge it before the Court under this procedure. There is no mention of directives in the list, but it has been argued before the CJEU that directives are decisions addressed to the Member States. Therefore they could come within (c) above. The main points which need to be resolved are to clarify what amounts to a "decision in the form of a regulatory act" and "direct and individual concern".

A decision in the form of a regulatory act

The title of the particular Union act is not decisive, therefore because it is called a "regulation" it will not automatically bar the action. It is the content and not the form that is important. A regulation under art.249 EC (ex 189 EC) is essentially of a legislative nature and is applicable to a number of persons viewed abstractly and in their entirety. In the *Fruit & Vegetables* case the Court held that "a measure which is applicable to objectively determined situations and which involves immediate legal consequences in all Member States for categories of persons viewed in a general and abstract manner cannot be considered as constituting a decision".

A regulation does not lose its character as a regulation simply because it may be possible to ascertain the number or even the identity of the persons to which it applies at any given time (see Case 6/68 *Zuckerfabrik Watenstedt v Council* and Case 789/79 *Calpak SpA v Commission*). In Case 25/62 *Plaumann & Co v EEC Commission* the CJEU stated that "it follows from Articles 249 EC and 254 EC (ex 189 and 191 EC) that decisions are characterised by the limited number of persons to whom they are addressed".

If the CJEU concludes that the act is a true regulation then it cannot be challenged under art.230 EC, but the individual may seek a remedy within their national courts.

Direct and individual concern

The inclusion of this phrase in the article has severely restricted the possibilities for it to be used by an individual who is seeking to challenge a decision not addressed to them.

Direct concern This is interpreted by the Court to mean that the addressee is left no latitude of discretion so that the decision affects the applicant without the addressee being required to take any decision himself. In the *Toepfer* case mentioned below on p.85 the applicant was directly concerned because the decision was addressed to the German government, who could not alter its application. When the Japanese companies challenged the Community rules on ball bearings the action was admissible because the national implementing measures were purely automatic (see *Japanese Ball-Bearing* cases, e.g. Cases 113/77 and 119–121/77).

In the Chinese Mushrooms case (Case 62/70 *Werner A. Bock v EC Commission*) the fact that the German authorities had already made up their mind to reject the applicant's request when they had authorisation to do so from the Commission, made the matter of direct concern to the applicant.

The notion of direct concern has some similarities with that of direct effect. In both cases the government of the Member State has no discretion and the act is of legal relevance to individuals who need not be the addressee of the decision.

KEY CASE

CASE C-25/62 PLAUMANN V COMMISSION

Facts: Plaumann one of 30 German importers of clementines who brought an action against a refusal by the Commission to grant a request by the Federal Republic of Germany for permission to suspend the customs duties on the import of fresh clementines from non-EC countries. The refusal by the Commission had been made in a decision under the now repealed art.25(3) **EC.** The implication for Plaumann was that it had to pay a customs duty of 13%, whereas the German Government had asked the Commission to reduce the duty to 10%. The Commission contested the case by claiming that it was inadmissible under art.263 **TFEU** (then art.173(2) **EC**) because the decision addressed to the government of a Member State was of a special nature and therefore not susceptible to challenge by private persons. It also said that Plaumann was not directly and individually concerned. Thus, the argument before the Court concentrated on this issue of inadmissibility.

Held: The Court accepted that art.263 **TFEU** (then art.173(2) **EC**) does allow an individual to bring an action against decisions addressed to another person if they are of direct and individual concern, but the Article neither defines nor limits the scope of these words. The words should be given their natural meaning and the broadest interpretation. As the provision provides a right for interested parties to bring an action, it must not be interpreted restrictively. Therefore, the Commission's argument was not considered to be well founded.

On the question of 'direct and individual' concern, the Court decided to look at whether the applicant was individually concerned, because if the answer is negative it will be unnecessary to inquire whether he is directly concerned. On this question of 'individually concerned', the decision must affect applicants by reason of certain attributes which are peculiar to them, or there must be certain circumstances which differentiate them from all other persons. As a result of these factors, the applicant is distinguished individually, just as if they were the person to whom the decision was addressed.

The decision affects Plaumann as an importer of clementines, a commercial activity which may be practised by any person. Thus, he is not distinguished sufficiently to show individual concern. Therefore, the Court declared the action for annulment to be inadmissible on the second point put forward by the Commission.

Commentary: The main importance of this case was concerned with whether Plaumann could challenge this decision by the Commission. It was open to the German Government to challenge the decision because it was addressed to them. But could Plaumann as a 'private individual' bring the matter before the CJEU? An action for annulment can be brought under art.263 TFEU, but as far as individuals are concerned this Article has been restrictively interpreted by the Court. It is possible to challenge a decision addressed to oneself, but if it is addressed to another, the applicant must show that it is of direct and individual concern to them. This case was followed by a number of cases decided on a similar basis, to the detriment of the applicants.

However, in the first *Toepfer* case (C-106 & 107/63) a decision addressed to the German government was considered to be of individual concern to the applicant. In this case the number of importers involved was in the past and therefore fixed as no new names could be added to the list. The Court said that the facts "differentiates the said importers ... from all other persons and distinguishes them individually just as in the case of the person addressed" (see also Case 100/74 *CAM SA v EC Commission* (the CAM case)).

It would appear from the case law of the Court that a natural or legal person can only claim to be individually concerned when he disputes an act concerning a period in the past and which affects an identifiable group of persons, to which the applicant belongs.

Despite statements in *Plaumann* that art.263 TFEU should not be interpreted too restrictively; the number of successful actions by private individuals where the decision is not addressed to them is very small. It was thought that perhaps the CJEU was in the process of changing this view (see Case 358/89 *Extramet Industrie v Council*) but recent judgments have reaffirmed the *Plaumann* judgment. In Case 50/00 *Union de Pequenos Agricultores v EC Council* Advocate-General Jacobs suggested that where an individual would have no other possible remedy, it was only just that their action should be heard under art.263 TFEU. This was followed by the Court of First Instance (now the General Court) in Case 177/01 *Jégo-Quéré et Cie SA v Commission* also supporting reform.

KEY CASE

CASE C-263/02 P COMMISSION V JÉGO-QUÉRÉ & CIE SA

Facts: The fishing company Jégo-Quéré & Cie, established in France, was involved in fishing mainly for whiting, to the south of Ireland. It used nets which were prohibited by a Commission regulation of 2001, the aim of which was to renew hake stocks. It brought an action before the General Court of the European Communities for annulment of two of the provisions of that regulation. The General Court held the action to be admissible and in doing this adopted a new definition of individual concern. The Commission appealed to the CJEU on the basis that the General Court had applied the wrong test.

Held: The CJEU reaffirmed its restrictive interpretation of art.263 **TFEU** in the *Plaumann* case and said that it was for national courts to provide a remedy. This could be achieved by the claimant indirectly challenging a regulation in an action before their national court or having raised the question of validity to ask that court to make a reference using the preliminary reference procedure under art.267 **TFEU**.

The CJEU set aside the judgment of the Court of First Instance (General Court) and declared the application for annulment by Jégo Quéré & Cie to be inadmissible.

Commentary: The CJEU are firm that there would need to be an amendment to the Treaties if individuals are to be able to able to challenge Union measures. Having overruled the judgment of the General Court the onus was put on the courts of the Member States to provide a remedy in such circumstances.

However, the Court of Justice reiterated in the judgment in *Union de Pequenos Agricultores* that the *Plaumann* test should apply and it was for the national courts to provide a remedy if the individual did not satisfy the test for an action under art.263 **TFEU**. However, if the individual can satisfy the test for locus standi they still have to prove one of the five grounds specified in the second paragraph of the article if the measure is to be annulled.

Grounds for annulment

The grounds for illegality must have been present at the time the decision was taken. There are five such grounds, although they have gradually lost their individual importance. The case law of the Court would seem to indicate that the CJEU is not concerned with the specific ground of illegality. The most common grounds pleaded are "infringement of this Treaty or of any rule of law relating to its application".

1. Lack of Competence—The institutions of the Community have no general powers and may only act where the Treaty expressly attributes competence to them. This idea is similar to that of ultra vires in English law.

2. Infringement of an essential Procedural requirement—For the purposes of annulment of an act three procedural requirements have been identified as essential. These are (a) that the required advice must have been sought, e.g. from the European Parliament; (b) the acts must be reasoned; and (c) the acts must have been published (see Case 139/79 *Maizena GmbH v EC Council* and Case 138/79 *SA Roquette Frere v EC Council* where the opinion of the European Parliament was not received before the Council acted. The result was that the measure was annulled).

3. Infringement of this Treaty—This is the most important ground as virtually any error by a Community institution can be viewed as a violation of the Treaty. Therefore this ground is the most widely used and is one which has been the most often successful.

4. Infringement of any rule of law relating to the application of this Treaty—The CJEU has stated that this includes all rules of EU law other than those found in the Treaty. It therefore includes all the general principles of Community law.

5. Misuse of Powers—Derived from French administrative law this ground covers those situations where a power is used for a purpose other than that for which it was granted, i.e. an improper purpose. Unlike the other grounds of invalidity, which are objective in character, the misuse of powers is subjective. It is therefore difficult to prove.

Time limits
Under art.263(5) TFEU proceedings must be instituted "within two months of the publication of the measure, or of its notification to the plaintiff, or, in the absence thereof, of the day on which it came to the knowledge of the latter, as the case may be."

Effect of the annulment
The remedy for actions under art.263 TFEU is stated in art.264 TFEU:

"If the action is well founded, the Court of Justice shall declare the act concerned to be void. However, the Court shall, if it considers this necessary, state which of the effects of the act which it has declared void shall be considered as definitive".

Thus the measure will be declared erga omnes, as if it never existed. Under art.233 TFEU the institution whose act has been declared void must take the necessary measures to comply with the judgment of the Court. If the successful applicant has suffered financial loss he may seek damages under art.340(2) TFEU.

Action for failure to act

This action, which is often called the appeal against inaction, is founded upon art.265 TFEU. Although it is rarely used, its potential use is against the Council or Commission and the European Parliament. As with art.263 TFEU mentioned above there are the two classes of applicant, the privileged and the non-privileged. The article requires that the defaulting institution must first be called upon to act. If after two months the institution concerned has not defined its position, the action may be brought after a further two months. The remedy for the action is contained in art.266 TFEU, i.e. the institution should act.

The CJEU has concluded that the obvious similarities between art.263 and 265 TFEU mean that the two articles are concerned essentially with the same remedy. This is referred to as the "unity principle". Therefore an individual cannot use one against the other. For example in the first *Lutticke* case the applicant invoked art.265 TFEU and called upon the Commission to initiate proceedings against the German government under art.258 TFEU. When they replied that there was no violation of art.110 TFEU by Germany, Lutticke brought an action under art.263 TFEU to have the reply annulled. The Court said that neither action was admissible as the Commission's reply was not a reviewable act and that by sending it they had acted so art.265 TFEU did not apply. Also in Case 289/97 *Eridania SpA v Azienda Agricola San Luca di Rumagnoli Viannj*, the applicant failed under art.263 TFEU because he was not directly and individually concerned. He asked for the acts to be repealed and when after two months they had not been he brought an action under art.265 TFEU. The Court refused to consider art.265 TFEU because it would have allowed the applicant to circumvent the conditions of art.263 TFEU.

Plea of illegality

The plea of illegality under art.277 TFEU is designed to prevent the application of an illegal act from being used as a legal basis for further action. It specifically refers to the fact that it applies when the time period mentioned in art.263(5) TFEU would otherwise bar an action. The article refers to "any party" being able to plead illegality, which would include both privileged and non-privileged applicants discussed above. Thus art.277 TFEU does not give a right of action in itself, but can be pleaded in other actions, such as annulment or failure to act or those for damages under art.340(2) TFEU.

The article refers specifically to "any proceedings in which an act of general application adopted by an institution, body, office or agency of the Union is at issue", so under the definitions in art.288 TFEU this would mean a regulation. However, as with art.263 TFEU above, the Court is concerned with the substance rather than the form. Article 277 TFEU is very rarely used because it can only be pleaded in actions before the CJEU or the General Court, which have very narrow locus standi for non-privileged applicants. It is not necessary to use the plea in domestic proceedings as under art.267(1)(b) TFEU the validity of a Union a ct, including regulations, can be raised.

Remedies available before the national courts

A request for a preliminary ruling on the validity of a Union act can be brought by national courts when they have to apply a Union act whose validity is doubted. This is done under the procedure of art.267(1)(b) TFEU. It obviates the situation where national courts would otherwise be obliged to apply invalid rules of Community law. However, the CJEU refused in Case 188/92 *TWD Textilwerke Deggendorf GmbH v Germany* to declare on the validity of a Commission decision because the applicants had been informed by the German government of their rights of challenge under art.263 TFEU.

As was held by the Court in Case 479/93 *Francovich v Italian Republic* it is also possible to obtain damages in the national courts (see Ch.4 above, p.54).

Damages under article 340 TFEU

Article 268 TFEU gives the CJEU exclusive jurisdiction to hear cases relating to compensation for tortious damage under art.340(2) TFEU. The contractual liability of the Union is governed by the law applicable to the contract in question.

The Court is instructed to decide cases of tortious liability in accordance with the general principles common to the laws of the Member States. In this way it is intended to make good any damage caused by Union institutions or by its servants in the performance of their duties. Unfortunately, the Court has adopted a very restrictive approach towards the tortious liability of the Community, although there have been some successes (see Case 145/83 *Adams v Commission*). Liability under art.340(2) TFEU can extend to liability in respect of legislation. Case 5/71 *Zuckerfrabrik Schoppenstedt v Council* developed certain guidelines for such situations. The court said that the non-contractual liability of the Union presupposes at the very least the unlawful nature of the act alleged to be the cause of the damage.

CASE C-5/71 AKTIEN-ZUCKERFABRIK SCHÖPPENSTEDT v COUNCIL

Facts: The undertaking *Aktien-Zuckerfabrik Schoppenstedt* brought an action in 1971 on the basis of Art 340 (2) **TFEU** (then art.215(2) **EC**), claiming damages from the Council caused by Regulation 769/68. This regulation laid down the measures needed to offset the difference between national sugar prices. The European Court of Justice has jurisdiction in disputes relating to compensation for damage by art.268 **TFEU**. However, this jurisdiction is linked to art.340 **TFEU**, which states that, in the case of non-contractual liability, the Union shall make good any damage caused by its institutions. The case is to be judged in accordance with the general principles common to the laws of the Member States.

The Council contested the admissibility of the application on the grounds that the applicant was claiming compensation for the removal of the legal effects arising from the contested regulation and not for any wrongful act or omission. Secondly, if the action was recognised as admissible it would undermine art.263 **TFEU** (then art.173 **EC**), under which individuals are not entitled to bring applications for the annulment of regulations.

Held: On the substance of the case, the Court said that the non-contractual liability of the EU presupposes at the very least the unlawful nature of the act alleged to be the cause of the damage. No non-contractual liability involving measures of economic policy will arise unless a sufficiently flagrant violation of a superior rule of law for the protection of the individual has occurred. Having set this principle, the Court had to decide whether such a violation had actually occurred in this case.

Commentary: The Court said that the term 'a superior rule of law for the protection of individuals' includes any general principle of EU law. This would include such examples as equality or proportionality. The applicants contended that by adopting different criteria for the right of compensation of sugar producers, the regulation infringed the then art.37(3) EC. However, the Court rejected this argument, as prices must be governed by market forces. Therefore, the applicant's action failed on the substance, because the condition mentioned above was not satisfied. The impact of the case has been the test set by the Court in actions under art.340 **TFEU** in the field of legislative economic policy. Cases which have followed have been regularly rejected.

The requirement that there should be a "sufficiently flagrant" or serious violation has been narrowly construed by the court. In the joined Cases 83 and 94/76 and 4, 15 and 40/77 of *Bayerische HNL Vermehrungsbetriebe GmbH v Council and Commission* the court stated that no liability would be incurred by the Union institutions unless the institution concerned had manifestly and gravely disregarded the limits on the exercise of its power. In subsequent cases the court's view has been that the breach must be both serious and inexcusable. See C-46 and C-48/93 *Brasserie du Pecheur & Factortame* joined cases.

Limitation period

Actions under art.340(2) TFEU are subject to a limitation period of five years.

REVISION CHECKLIST

You should now know and understand:

- [ ] the procedure for enforcement actions under arts 258, 259 and 260 TFEU
- [ ] the calculation of fines and penalties under art.263 TFEU
- [ ] the action for annulment under art.263 TFEU
- [ ] the problems for non-privileged applicants
- [ ] the meaning of direct and individual concern
- [ ] the grounds for annulment
- [ ] the action for failure to act under art.265 TFEU
- [ ] the plea of illegality
- [ ] remedies available before the national courts

SUMMARY OF KEY CASES

Case	Court	Key Principle
C-145/83 Adams v Commission)	CJEU	The CJEU has adopted a very restrictive interpretation of the tortuous liability of the Union—although Adams was successful.

C-4/69 Alfons Lutticke GmbH v E.C. Commission No.1	CJEU	Purpose of the Reasoned Opinion is to set out the facts and the EU law and inform the MS of the measures necessary to comply.
C-83 and 94/76 and 4, 15 and 40/77 of Bayerische HNL Vermehrungsbetriebe GmbH v Council and Com- mission	CJEU	No liability for Union institutions unless they had acted manifestly and gravely in disregard of their powers—i.e. serious and inexcusable.
C-789/79 Calpak SpA v Commission	CJEU	Because of their nature genuine Regulations can never be subject to challenge by individual applicant.
C-100/74 CAM SA v EC Commission	CJEU	CJEU considered the question of 'individual concern' by looking at the 'closed category test' and decided that the application was admissible.
C-26/69 Commission v France	CJEU	Advocate General Roemer suggested some situations where the Commission would be justified in not brining enforcement action.
C-304/02 Commission v French Republic	CJEU	CJEU ordered France to pay both a lump sum and a periodic penalty payment for breach of EU law.
C-387/97 Commission v Greece	CJEU	First case where CJEU imposed both a lump sum and a periodical penalty payment under the TEU.
C-7/61 Commission v Italy (Pork Imports case)	CJEU	The action is not terminated because the breach ends before the judgment of the Court is given.

C-45/93 Commission v Spain	CJEU	Member States have a legal duty to cooperate with Commission investigations.
C-128/78 Commission v UK	CJEU	Trade Union opposition is not an excuse for failure by a Member State to comply with EU legislation.
C-22/70 EC Commission v EC Council (the ERTA case)	CJEU	The CJEU reviewed the legality of an agreement entered into by some Member States.
C-70/88 European Parliament v Council (the Chernobyl case)	CJEU	The EP could use the judicial review procedure to protect its prerogatives—now listed in art.263 TFEU.
C-289/97 Eridania SpA v Azienda Agricola San Luca di Rumagnoli Viannj	CJEU	Applicants have to be directly and individually concerned under art.263 TFEU.
C-141/78 France v UK	CJEU	France showed that the UK rules on the mesh size of fishing nets were contrary to EU law.
C-479/93 Francovich v Italian Republic	CJEU	CJEU extended the principle of State liability.
C-177/01 Jégo-Quéré et Cie SA v Commission	General Court (previously the CFI)	General Court seeking to assist the applicants (by giving a wider interpretation to 'direct & individual concern' had judgment reversed by CJEU.
C-224/01 Kobler v Austria	CJEU	Breach of EU law by national court may make the state liable in damages.
C-294/83 Les Verts v Parliament	CJEU	The EP could bring action for annulment but only on limited grounds—now covered by art.263 TFEU.

C-25/62 Plaumann & Co v EEC Commission	CJEU	Plaumann one of 30 German importers so could not show 'individual concern'–test developed from this case.
C-188/92 TWD Textilwerke Deggendorf GmbH v Germany	CJEU	CJEU refused to declare on 'validity' of Commission decision where art.263 TFEU should be used.
C-50/00 Union de Pequenos Agricultores v EC Council	CJEU	Plaumann test to be applied and for national courts to provide a remedy for those who fail the test.
C-62/70 Werner A. Bock v EC Commission	CJEU	Direct concern was identified because the German authorities had already made up its mind to reject Bock's application–making him part of a closed category.
C-5/71 Zuckerfrabrik Schoppenstedt v Council	CJEU	CJEU laid down criteria for determining fault.
C-6/68 Zuckerfabrik Watenstedt v Council	CJEU	Regulation does not lose its character as a regulation simply because the number or identity or persons can be identified.
C-106 & 107/63 Toepfer v Commission	CJEU	The decision successfully challenged by Toepfer involved a fixed list of importers that could not be changed and the national authorities had no discretion.

QUESTION AND ANSWER

QUESTION

How and in what circumstances may an individual use art.263 TFEU to challenge a measure of EU law?

Introduction—The ability to bring an action before the CJEU or the General Court for judicial review has been severely restricted by the CJEU's interpretation of art.263 TFEU as far as non-privileged applicants are concerned. Only the Community institutions as privileged applicants are able to challenge any Community act.

Individuals can only challenge a Union act in certain circumstances. If a Decision is addressed to them, as may happen under competition law, they may challenge it. However if it is not addressed to them but is a decision addressed to someone else (*Werner A. Bock v EC Commission*) or in the form of a regulation (*CAM SA v EC Commission*) it has to be of direct and individual concern to the applicant if they are going to be able to challenge it.

This is where the CJEU has been very restrictive in its interpretation (*Union de Pequenos Agricultores v EC Council*) and held that the case of *Plaumann & Co v EEC Commission* provided the best interpretation that should be followed.

The challenge under art.263 TFEU must be brought within the time limit of two months and even if the challenge is heard by the Court the individual still has to prove one of the grounds specified in art.263(2) TFEU if they are to succeed.

Free Movement of Goods

7

INTRODUCTION

To many the term "common market" is used to describe what the European Union is all about. The association with trade and the free movement of goods is what promoted the ideas to the forefront of the development of the Union in the 1950s and encouraged the UK to apply for membership in the 1960s. However, although the Union has developed other priorities the free movement of goods is still a fundamental principle. This chapter reviews the law on this topic.

An essential element of the common market is the series of freedoms which constitute the "foundations of the Union". Of these freedoms the most important is the free movement of goods which also includes agricultural products.

The Treaty does not provide a definition of the concept "common market", but art.28(1) TFEU states that:

> "The Union shall comprise a customs union which shall cover all trade in goods and which shall involve the prohibition between Members States of customs duties on imports and exports and of all charges having equivalent effect, and the adoption of a common customs tariff in their relations with third countries."

The latter differentiates between a customs union and a free trade area, such as NAFTA, which has no common customs tariff and is therefore limited to free movement of products originating in states belonging to the trade area.

The customs union was completed on June 30, 1968 for the original Member States. It was given effect by two essential measures:
1. abolition of customs duties between Member States, and
2. full application of the common customs tariff.

In order to create a single internal market of the whole Union it was necessary to remove the economic frontiers and legal obstacles to transnational trade. In theory the operation was based on the twin principles of free circulation of goods and non-discrimination between domestic and foreign products of the Member States. In that sense exports and imports as between Member

States has become only a matter of domestic accounting as far as individual Member States are concerned. In fact the Commission now collects the information on trade. In practice the CJEU initially insisted on the enforcement of both principles, but seems now to be content to enforce the principle of free circulation which was given a broad meaning. On the question of non-discrimination the CJEU seems more concerned with cases involving internal trading between the Member States.

Thus the Treaty envisages the Community based on a Customs Union. This concept rests upon arts 28 and 110 TFEU.

Article 28 TFEU—enumerates the elements necessary to achieve a customs union.
Article 110 TFEU—prohibits internal taxation on imports having an equivalent effect to customs duties.

CHECKPOINT

Free circulation
Goods benefiting from the right to free circulation are the products originating from Member States as well as products coming from non-Member States which are in free circulation in that Member State.

"Products coming from a third country shall be considered to be in free circulation in a Member State if the import formalities have been complied with and any customs duties or charges having equivalent effect which are payable have been levied in that Member State" art.29 TFEU.

Elimination of duties between Member States

This was a formidable task because it was not merely a question of clearing up the jungle of national customs laws but basically of overcoming the idea of Member States being sovereign economic units. To ensure an immediate effect art.30 TFEU prohibits the increase of existing customs duties and the imposition of new duties on imports and exports or any charges having an equivalent effect (see *Van Gend en Loos*).

Charges having equivalent effect

While the illegality of customs duties, export taxes and levies is a straightforward proposition "charges having an equivalent effect" prohibited by art.30 TFEU have posed a continuous problem as they are often subtle in execution. Although they are not defined by the Treaty, the CJEU defined these charges as:

"... duties whatever their description or techniques imposed unilaterally, which apply specifically to a product imported by a Member State, but not to a similar national product and which by altering the price, have the same effect upon the free movement of goods as a customs duty" (Case 24/68 *Commission v Italy*).

Examples

(a) A statistical levy on imported goods—Case 7/68 *EC Commission v Italy*.

(b) A tax on cardboard egg containers charged to egg importer for the benefit of a national organisation set up for the promotion of production of paper and cellulose in Italy (Case 94/74 *Industria Gomma v Ente Nazionale per la Cellulose*).

Both (a) and (b) are prohibited by the Treaty.

(c) Charging 0.50 per cent ad valorem duty for administrative services in respect of goods imported from other MS. Italy was found to be guilty of a failure to fulfil an obligation under the Treaty.

(d) More plausible charges such as for phyto-sanitary inspection of fruit or veterinary and public health inspection of meat are also prohibited unless authorised by the Community and applied accordingly.

It is not the test that is disapproved of but the charge for the test. It would appear from the case law of the Court that a charge levied for a service rendered to the importer and which is not too general and uncertain would be permissible. This principle has, however, been given the narrowest possible scope. The CJEU has held that where an inspection service is imposed in the general interest, e.g. for health or safety purposes or quality control, this cannot be regarded as a service rendered to the importer or exporter to justify the imposition of a charge.

Article 110 TFEU

Similar to customs duties and equivalent charges are internal taxes which if imposed upon goods coming from a fellow Member State would discriminate against such goods. Such taxes are prohibited by art.110 TFEU if they are in excess of taxes imposed upon similar domestic products. For example, a German importer of powdered milk was able to resist the demand for a payment in lieu of a turnover tax from which a similar national product was exempted (see also *Commission v France* (C-168/78) and *Commission v Greece* (C-230/89)).

Elimination of quantitative restriction

Having abolished customs duties the Treaty purports to eliminate quotas by prohibiting quantitative restrictions on imports (art.34 TFEU) and exports (art.35 TFEU). Quantitative restrictions have been interpreted by the CJEU "as any measure which amounts to a total or partial restraint on imports, exports or goods in transit" (see Case 2/73 *Riseria Luigi Geddo v Ente Nazionale Risi*). There are still problems with Member States acting independently to manipulate trade for domestic reasons. In law they can no longer resort to protectionist measures either to regulate the influx of foreign goods as a matter of national policy or to respond to pressures from industries incapable of coping with foreign competition. There were many examples initially but it is now rare for countries to resort to quotas, e.g. UK potatoes, French sheep meat. However, covert quota systems might operate by means of an import licence requirement. A licensing system might in itself amount to a quantitative restriction or, alternatively, a measure of equivalent effect to a quantitative restriction. Even if the granting of the licence was a pure formality the requirement of such a licence to import would amount to a breach of art.34 TFEU. To offer States guidance as to the meaning and scope of "measures having equivalent effect" to quantitative restrictions the Commission passed Directive 70/50. Although this Directive was concerned with the transitional period of the Community and therefore no longer binding, it does offer a non-binding guideline as to the measures to be considered as having equivalent effect.

There are "measures equivalent to quantitative restrictions" prohibited but not defined by the Treaty. To the surprise of Member States, both the Commission and the CJEU have been very generous in their interpretation of this term, to include not merely overtly protective measures or measures applicable only to imports (i.e. distinctly applicable measures), but measures applicable to imports and domestic goods alike (indistinctly applicable measures), often introduced for the best of motives. Such measures range from regulatory measures designed to enforce minimum standards, e.g. of size, weight, quality, price or content, to tests and inspections or certification requirements to ensure that goods conform to these standards, to any activity capable of influencing the behaviour of traders such as promoting goods by reason of their national origin (Case 113/80 *Commission v Ireland* (the Buy Irish Campaign Case).

Dassonville formula

In 1974 the CJEU had the opportunity in *Dassonville* (the Scotch whisky case) to provide its own definition of measures having equivalent effect to quantitative restrictions. This definition, known as the *Dassonville* formula, has since been applied consistently. According to the formula:

"All trading rules enacted by Member States which are capable of hindering, directly or indirectly, actually or potentially, intra-Community trade are to considered as measures having effect equivalent to quantitative restrictions."

Thus it is not necessary to show actual effect on trade between Member States as long as the measure is capable of such effects.

The measure in issue in *Dassonville* was a requirement, under Belgian law, that imported goods should carry a certificate of origin issued by the State in which the goods were manufactured. Dassonville imported a consignment of Scotch whisky from France. Since the sellers were unable to supply the required certificate he attached a homemade certificate of origin to the goods and appeared before the Belgian court on a forgery charge. In his defence, he claimed that the Belgian regulation was contrary to EC law. On a reference from the Belgian court under art.267 TFEU, the CJEU, applying the above formula, found that the measure was capable of breaching art.34 TFEU.

KEY CASE

CASE 120/78 REWE-ZENTRAL AG V BUNDESMONOPOLVERWALTUNG FUR BRANNTWEIN (THE CASSIS DE DIJON CASE)

The CJEU took another decisive step in the case of *Cassis de Dijon* (Case 120/78 *Rewe-Zentral AG v Bundesmonopolverwaltung für Branntwein*). This made a distinction between distinctly and indistinctly applicable measures. The question before the CJEU concerned the legality under EU law of a German law laying down a minimum alcohol level of 25 per cent for certain spirits, which included cassis, a blackcurrant-flavoured liqueur. German cassis complied with this minimum, but French cassis, with an alcohol content of 15–20 per cent did not. Thus although the German regulation was indistinctly applicable, the result of the mea- sure was effectively to ban French cassis from the German market. A number of German importers contested the measure, and the German court referred a number of questions to the CJEU under art.267 TFEU.

The CJEU applied the *Dassonville* formula above but added: "Obstacles to movement within the Community resulting from disparities between the national laws relating to the marketing of the products in question must be accepted in so far as those provisions may be recognised as being necessary in order to satisfy mandatory requirements relating in particular to the effectiveness of fiscal supervision, the protection of public

> health, the fairness of commercial transactions and the defence
> of the consumer."
>
> **Commentary:** This has subsequently been called the first Cassis principle, i.e. that certain measures will not breach art.34 **TFEU** if they are necessary to satisfy mandatory requirements even though they may come within the *Dassonville* formula because they are indistinctly applicable. If the measure is distinctly applicable it will normally breach art.34 **TFEU** but may be justified under art.36 **TFEU**.

Thus in the *Cassis* case the CJEU found that the German law was in breach of art.34 **TFEU**. Although the measure was allegedly enacted in the interests of public health (to prevent increased consumption resulting from lowering the alcoholic content of cassis) and the fairness of commercial transactions (to avoid giving the weak imported cassis an unfair advantage over its stronger, hence more expensive German rival), the measure was not necessary to achieve these ends. Other means, such as labelling, which would have been less of a hindrance to trade, could have been used to achieve the same ends.

The CJEU established another important principle in the *Cassis* case ("the second Cassis principle"). "There was no valid reason why, provided that goods have been lawfully produced and marketed in one of the Member States, they should not be introduced into any other Member State." This gives rise to a presumption that goods which have been lawfully marketed in another Member State will comply with the "mandatory requirements" of the importing State. This can be rebutted by evidence that further measures are necessary to protect the interest concerned. However, the burden of proving that a measure is necessary is a heavy one and the presumption will be very hard to rebut.

Price controls, resulting in the fixing of profit margins, may be regarded as a measure having an equivalent effect to quantitative restrictions on imports if they place imported goods at a disadvantage in relation to identical national products/goods, e.g. a Dutch licensed victualler, prosecuted for selling liquor at prices below the minimum fixed by the national law, successfully raised a defence that the prosecution was contrary to art.34 **TFEU**.

KEY CASE

CASES C-267 AND 268/91 CRIMINAL PROCEEDINGS AGAINST KECK AND MITHOUARD

Keck and Mithouard were prosecuted in a French court under a law which prohibited the selling of goods at a price lower than its actual purchase price. The defendants claimed that such a prohibition was contrary to art.28 EC (now art.34 TFEU). The CJEU was concerned that traders were invoking art.34 TFEU where any national legislation affected their commercial operations and therefore they took the opportunity to make clear how such measures should be approached.

Held: The Court had consistently held that any measure which is capable of directly or indirectly, actually or potentially, hindering intra-Community (intra-Union) trade constitutes a measure having equivalent effect to a quantitative restriction. However, the *Dassonville* formula is wide and provided certain conditions are met such rules as in this case, which do not impede access to the market, are outside the scope of art.34 TFEU.

Commentary: *Keck* lays down a general rule that distinguishes between 'rules which relate to the goods themselves' such as packaging, etc. where Cassis would apply; and 'rules relating to selling arrangements' which do not fall within art.34 TFEU provided that conditions are met. These conditions are so long as those provisions 'apply to all relevant traders operating within the national territory and so long as they affect in the same manner, in law and in fact, the marketing of domestic products and of those from other Member States'.

The Court applied *Keck* in Case 391/92 *Commission v Greece*, a case involving the sale of processed milk for infants. Although the national legislation might restrict the volume of sales the legislation satisfied the conditions laid down in *Keck* and consequently did not breach art.34 TFEU. The recent judgment in Case 322/01 *Deutscher Apothekerverband* involving the prohibition of the sale of medicines on the internet by German law illustrates the application of *Keck* to modern situations. The prohibition was found to be contrary to art.34 TFEU, although there may be an argument for derogation under art.36 TFEU.

The recent judgements concerning 'access to the market' have shown how the Court can decide that the actions of Member State fall within the prohibitions of art.34 TFEU but then see if art.36 TFEU can be applied. In C-110/05 *Commission v Italy* (the 'trailer case') the Court held that the Italian government had acted unlawfully when prohibiting the importation of trailers designed to be used with motorcycles but said that such prohibition was 'justified by the public interest ground of ensuring road safety'. In case C-142/ 05 *Mickelsson and Roos* the CJEU held that Swedish rules on the use of jet-skis on navigable waterways were caught by the prohibition of measures hindering the free movement of goods in art.34 TFEU but could be justified under art.36 TFEU. In this reference under art.267 TFEU the Court said that it would up to the national court to decide if the criteria under art.36 TFEU had been met.

Derogation under article 36 TFEU

Article 36 TFEU allows Member States to legitimately limit the freedom of movement of goods and thus derogate from principles comprised in arts 34 and 35 TFEU. Although the grounds in art.36 TFEU appear extensive they have been narrowly construed by the Court. They must not constitute a means of arbitrary discrimination or a disguised restriction on trade between Member States.

The grounds for derogation are "public morality, public policy and public security; the protection of health and life of humans, animals or plants; the protection of national treasures possessing artistic, historic or archaeological value; or the protection of industrial and commercial property".

"Public morality, policy and security"

These terms express "peculiar national values" and it is difficult to envisage a uniform Community application of a diversity of values. The CJEU recog-nised its limitations in dealing with public policy and decreed that a certain margin of appreciation may be left to national authorities. However, it does not follow that these matters are reserved to the exclusive jurisdiction of Member States, but permits national law to derogate from the principle of free movement of goods to the extent that such derogation is and continues to be justified under art.36 TFEU.

Public morality Examples—compare pornographic material freely available in another Member State in *R. v Henn*, *R. v Darby* [1980] 2 All E.R. 166 with *Conegate Ltd v Customs & Excise Commissioners* [1987] Q.B. 254 which involved the seizure of a number of inflatable rubber love dolls imported from Germany.

Public policy This ground, potentially wide, has been strictly construed, and has only succeeded as a basis for derogation under art.36 TFEU on few occasions. One example is *R v Thompson and Others* (Case C-7/78) where the UK government prosecuted Thompson and others for importing gold coins to be melted down. The "public policy" at issue was the protection of the national coinage and the right to mint coinage.

Public security This ground was successfully invoked in Case 72/83 *Campus Oil Ltd v Minister for Industry and Energy* to justify an Irish order requiring importers of petroleum oils to buy up to 35 per cent of their requirements of petroleum products from the Irish National Petroleum Company at prices fixed by the minister. The Irish government argued that it was justified on public security grounds, to maintain a viable refinery that would meet essential needs in times of crisis. This was accepted by the CJEU.

Protection of public health

The cases reveal devices used by Member States to raise revenue or to discriminate against imported products. The health protection plea seems to have been argued rather tenuously and it was the commercial aspect which characterised those cases. However, it is possible to envisage a legitimate and compelling use in some cases such as those involving health precautions against rabies or humanitarian considerations in the transport of livestock.

There have been a number of attempts to derogate from the Treaty under this heading, e.g. *Commission v UK (Re UHT Milk)*, *Commission v UK (Re Imports of Poultry Meat)* and Case 42/82 *Commission v France (Re Italian Table Wines)*.

If a charge is levied for the inspection it may be considered as a charge having equivalent effect. If it is not prohibited by the Treaty and not seen as a way of raising revenue but actually seen to assist the flow of goods it may be acceptable.

Protection of industrial and commercial property

This includes patents, copyright and trademarks. Faced with the problem of such rights being used in order to frustrate the Community competition policy or to impede the free movement of goods the CJEU distinguished between the existence of rights and their use. Only a legitimate use, i.e. one that is compatible with the rules on competition and the free movement of goods is justified.

In the opinion of the Court:

"... in as much as it provides an exception to one of the fundamental principles of the Common Market, art.36 TFEU in fact admits exceptions to the free movement of goods only to the extent to which such exceptions are justified for the purpose of safeguarding rights which constitute the specific subject matter of that property" (Case 119/75 *Terrapin (Overseas) Ltd v Terranova Industrie* (see also Competition Policy in the next chapter)).

You should now know and understand:

- ☐ the meaning of the "common market" and a customs union
- ☐ the meaning of a quantitative restriction
- ☐ the meaning of "measures having equivalent effect"
- ☐ the *Dassonville* formula
- ☐ the impact of the *Cassis de Dijon* case
- ☐ the derogations under art.36 TFEU

SUMMARY OF KEY CASES

Case	Court	Key Principle
C-72/83 Campus Oil Ltd v Minister for Industry and Energy	CJEU	Public security used by the Irish government to justify requiring importers of petroleum to buy supplies from state refinery.
C-168/78 Commission v France	CJEU	The application of discriminatory taxation on spirits distilled from cereals and spirits obtained from wine and fruit is a breach of EU law.
C-42/82 Commission v France (Re Italian Table Wines)	CJEU	French legislation requiring imported Italian wine to be subjected to rigorous inspections was contrary to EU law.
C-230/89 Commission v Greece	CJEU	By applying to spirits a system of differentiated VAT rates discriminating against imported beverages which Greece does not produce they failed to fulfil obligations under art.95 EC (now art.114 TFEU).

C-391/92 Commission v Greece	CJEU	Greece prohibited the sale of processed milk for infants except from pharmacies but CJEU said that this was a 'selling arrangement' and not contrary to EU law.
C-113/80 Commission v Ireland	CJEU	The Irish claim that legislation was valid as consumer protection rejected because only applied to imported jewellery.
C-7/68 EC Commission v Italy	CJEU	CJEU gave wide definition to 'goods'–products that can be valued in money and which are capable of forming the subject of commercial transactions'.
C-24/68 Commission v Italy	CJEU	The charge must be payment for some tangible benefit to the importer.
C-110/05 Commission v Italy (the 'trailer case')	CJEU	CJEU recognised that Italian rules on trailers could be regarded as a measure having equivalent effect contrary to EU law but could be justified to protect road safety.
C-124/81 Commission v UK (Re UHT Milk),	CJEU	UK restriction on marketing of UHT milk not justified under art.36 TFEU and breached EU law.
C-40/82 Commission v UK (Re Imports of Poultry Meat)	CJEU	UK failed to justify restrictions on poultry imports to prevent spread of Newcastle disease.
C-121/85 Conegate Ltd v Customs & Excise Commissioners	CJEU	There must be no arbitrary discrimination against imports.
C-267 and C-268/91 Criminal Proceedings against Keck and Mithouard	CJEU	The CJEU said that there was a distinction between the law regulating the goods themselves and selling arrangements, ie where, when or how they were sold.

C-322/01 Deutscher Apothekerverband	CJEU	The German legislation was prima facie a breach of EU law subject to a justification under art.36 TFEU on health grounds.
C-142/05 Mickelsson and Roos	CJEU	Swedish legislation prohibiting the use of 'personal watercraft' justified on environmental protection grounds.
C-7/78 R. v Thompson and Others	CJEU	Old coins that are no longer legal tender are dealt with under the free movement of goods.
C-34/79 R. v Henn, R. v Darby	CJEU & House of Lords (now the Supreme Court)	Ban on pornographic books was a quantitative restriction and contrary to EU law.
C-120/78 Rewe-Zentral AG v Bundesmonopol-verwaltung fur Branntwein (The Cassis de Dijon case).	CJEU	'Obstacles to movement within the Union resulting from disparities between national laws relating to the marketing of products...maybe recognised as satisfying 'mandatory requirements'.
C-2/73 Riseria Luigi Geddo v Ente Nazionale Risi	CJEU	Quantitative restriction 'measures' which amount to a total or partial restraint of imports or exports'.
C-119/75 Terrapin (Overseas) Ltd v Terranova Industrie	CJEU	It is compatible with EU law relating to the free movement of goods for an undertaking in one MS with a protected trade-mark to prevent the importation of products of an undertaking established in another Member State bearing a name giving rise to confusion provided that there are no agreements contrary to competition law.

QUESTION AND ANSWER

QUESTION

Arthur Rose Ltd imported a consignment of plastic tulips into the UK from the Netherlands and was required to have each flower individually tested to ensure that it conformed to a new test for imported plastic products. The company wishes to challenge this requirement on the ground that it is incompatible with European Union law. Advise Arthur.

ADVICE AND THE ANSWER

Introduction—this problem question concerns the free movement of goods. The EU is based upon a customs union (art.28 TFEU) which requires a common external tariff and the removal of all barriers to intra-Community trade. As these tulips are being imported from another Member State (the Netherlands) these principles should apply here.

Article 34 TFEU states that all barriers to trade which amount to quantitative restrictions and all measures having equivalent effect are prohibited. (*Riseria Luigi Geddo v Ente Nazionale Risi*.) The CJEU has given the concept a wide interpretation by dividing it into measures which are indistinctly applicable and those which are distinctly applicable, the latter being those which only apply to imported goods. The main case law on this can be found in the cases of *Dassonville* (1974) and *Cassis de Dijon* (1987). These cases developed the *Dassonville* formula which states that all trading rules enacted by Member States which are capable of hindering intra-community trade are to be considered to be as measures having an effect equivalent to quantitative restrictions. However, art.34 TFEU will not be breached if the requirements can satisfy a public interest such as the protection of public health. There is a presumption under the *Cassis de Dijon* second principle that goods lawfully marketed in one Member State will comply with the mandatory requirements of the importing Member State.

The advice to Arthur is that the requirements imposed by the UK for testing are applicable to imported goods only so the measure would be considered as a distinctly applicable one. As the goods are sold in the Netherlands the second principle from the *Cassis de Dijon* case would seem to apply. The best way for Arthur to proceed would be for him to bring an action in the national court and then ask for a request for a preliminary reference to be made by the court to the CJEU.

Competition Policy

8

INTRODUCTION

This chapter follows the discussion of the free movement of goods because it was felt that if trade restrictions by governments were to be removed they were not to be replaced by business creating their own barriers. This chapter reviews the law that has been developed to deal with anti-competitive activity by a few businesses working together or by one large business exercising what could be called monopolistic power.

ROLE OF COMPETITION IN THE EUROPEAN UNION

From its very beginning the European Community (now the Union) has always accorded great importance to competition. In art.3 TEU, where the principles or aims of the Union are listed, art.3(3) refers to a "highly competitive social market economy" and then in art.3(1)(b) TFEU it states that the Union shall have exclusive competence in the "establishing of the competition rules necessary for the functioning of the internal market".

This emphasis on competition has two advantages. For the European Commission competition is the best stimulant of economic activity as it guarantees the widest possible freedom of action to all. Second, it prevents the introduction within the internal market of any new obstacles to trade by individuals, undertakings or Member States now that old barriers have been removed. A strong competition policy can be used to fulfil the objectives of the Community, such as economic integration.

The Treaty does not define the concept of "competition", but it does refer to certain measures which interfere with competition and which are therefore prohibited, subject to exemptions granted by the Commission.

There are two dimensions to competition policy within a Member State; that of the national laws of the Member State and imposed upon that a system of Union law. The European Union rules are administered and enforced by the national authorities, subject to the special role of the Commission in the field of competition policy. Good communications between the Commission and the national authorities are important to ensure uniformity and to avoid the danger of concurrent national and Union action. If the

Commission takes action under the Union's competition rules, it has priority over any subsequent action taken in the national courts. Actions are brought before the General Court with a possible appeal on a point of law to the CJEU.

Article 101 TFEU and restrictive practices

Article 101 TFEU complements art.102 TFEU as they both seek to secure fair competition by curbing restraints on trade. The procedure for the application of these two articles is set out in Regulation 1/2003, which replaced Regulation 17/62. Article 101 TFEU is concerned with the effect on trade of various restrictive practices involving two or more undertakings, while art.102 TEU is primarily concerned with monopolist situations. Both are concerned with the abuse rather than the existence of economic power. The European Union claims extra-territorial jurisdiction in that even if the undertaking is established outside the EU the competition policy will still apply if its actions will affect trade between the Member States.

TREATY HIGHLIGHTER

ARTICLE 101 TFEU

1. The following shall be prohibited as incompatible with the common market: all agreements between undertakings, decisions by associations of undertakings and concerted practices which may affect trade between Member States and which have as their object or effect the prevention restrictions or distortion of competition within the common market, and in particular those which:

   (a) directly or indirectly fix purchase or selling prices or any other trading conditions;
   (b) limit or control production, markets, technical development, or investment;
   (c) share markets or sources of supply;
   (d) apply dissimilar conditions to equivalent transactions with other trading parties, thereby placing them at a competitive disadvantage; and
   (e) make the conclusion of contracts subject to acceptance by the other parties of supplementary obligations which, by their nature or according to commercial usage, have no connection with the subject of such contracts.

2. Any agreements or decisions prohibited pursuant to this article shall be automatically void.

3. The provisions of para.1 may, however, be declared inapplicable in the case of:

  — any agreement or category of agreements between
    undertakings;
  — any decision or category of decisions by associations of
    undertakings; or
  — any concerted practice or category of concerted practices;
which contributes to improving the production or distribution of goods
or to promoting technical or economic progress, while allowing consumers a fair share of the resulting benefit, and which does not;
  (a) impose on the undertakings concerned restrictions which are
      not indispensable to the attainment of these objects; and
  (b) afford such undertakings the possibility of eliminating compe-
      tition in respect of a substantial part of the products in
      question.

Agreements and Concerted Practices There are clearly three parts to
art.101 TFEU. Article 101(1) TFEU is concerned with agreements between
undertakings and decisions by associations of undertakings. However, it
goes further by the use of the term "concerted practices". This refers to
behaviour and includes any "gentleman's agreement" which has not been
put into writing. The Court defined concerted practices in Case 48/69 *ICI v
Commission* (the *Dyestuffs* case) as "a form of co-ordination between
enterprises that has not yet reached the point where there is a contract in the
true sense of the word but which, in practice consciously substitutes a
practical co-operation for the risks of competition". It may be that the simi-
larity of actions by undertakings is coincidental, in which case they are not
prohibited. It is only where they are planned as a result of some collusion or
concentration that they are prohibited. The Commission does have problems
in proving such arrangements where the evidence may be circumstantial.
However, the onus may be on the undertakings to prove that they had not
entered into such an arrangement (*Dyestuffs*). Article 101 TFEU is not concerned with agreements between undertakings belonging to the same concern, such as a parent company and its subsidiaries. A business must have
economic independence in order to qualify as an undertaking within art.101
TFEU (see Joined Cases 159/91 and 160/91 *Poucet v AGF*).

Whatever behaviour or agreement is involved the prohibition under this
article will not apply unless it has as its object or effect the prevention,
restrictions or distortion of competition within the "common market". This
can arise when any kind of action by an undertaking directly affects the
market and is detrimental to production or sales to purchasers or consumers
because it limits freedom of choice. The CJEU has refined the meaning of
distortion of competition by adding the phrase "to an appreciable extent". In
this way the Court has shown that it is not really concerned with small affects

by applying the de minimus rule. It is necessary under the guidelines from the Court to take into account the nature and quantity of the product covered by the agreement, the position and importance of the parties on the market for the products concerned, the isolated nature of the disputed agreement, the severity of the clauses limiting trade between Member States and the opportunities for commercial competition in the same product. The term "within the Union" does not necessarily refer to competition in several Member States or even all. If there is an adverse effect on competition in one single Member State it may be considered as taking place within the Union and prohibited by the article. There is also listed (a) to (e) examples of such behaviour or agreements.

KEY CASE

CASES 56 & 58/64 CONSTEN & GRUNDIG V COMMISSION

Facts: In this case attempts were made by private traders to carve up the internal market in the face of one of the fundamental objectives of the EU: the removal of national barriers to trade. Consten was a French firm of wholesalers for electrical products. Grundig was a German firm which manufactured radios, television sets and similar products in Germany. The reason the two cases are joined is because they both arose from the exclusive distribution contract made between the two businesses in 1957. Under this contract, Grundig promised not to deliver to any other French distributor and to include in any contract they entered into with other firms elsewhere a clause preventing their goods from being transferred to France. Consten promised in return to buy Grundig's products, and not from any other competitors, and not to deliver outside France. One final fact was that the products subject to the contract all carried the trade mark GINT, that is, Grundig International. Consten registered this mark in France with Grundig's consent.

When **Regulation 17/62** (now **Regulation 1/2003**) came into force the Commission took ma decision addressed to Grundig and Consten stating that their contract was in breach of art.101(1) **TFEU** (then art.85(1) EC). The firms challenged that decision which they did using art.263 **TFEU** (then art.173 EC) to bring an action for annulment before the CJEU.

Held: The Court's view was that the GINT trade mark was intended to place an obstacle in the way of parallel imports. As the agreement was void under art.101 (then art.85(2)) it would be ineffective if the trade mark could still be used by Consten to achieve the same objective. There is a distinction between the rights inherent in a trade mark, which are recognised by art.345, and the exercise of those rights. The rights of the owner of a trade mark are limited, to the extent that the exercise of those rights may infringe art.101.

Commentary: This early case in the application of the competition law shows how the Commission, supported by the Court, took as one of its fundamental task to ensure that individual companies did not work together to impose barriers. The Treaties are clear on the objective that the EU seeks to achieve and the Commission has the responsibility to enforce competition law.

Exemption: Article 101(2) TFEU states quite clearly that anything prohibited by art.101(1) TFEU is automatically void. However, art.101(3) TFEU provides for the possibility of exemption. Exemption in individual cases are no longer given by the Commission as this was considered too time consuming given the detailed investigation that had to be undertaken. The emphasis now is for a number of 'block exemptions' to be provided and these have been issued in the form of regulations. These cover such commercial activities as exclusive purchasing agreements, exclusive agency agreements, patent licensing and research, and development agreements. If the undertakings can ensure that the clauses of the agreement are within that specified by the block exemption they will not risk being fined and do not need to notify the Commission of the agreement. The pressure is on the individual undertakings to make their own assessment; the Commission may consider that the way that the agreement is being operated includes an element of anti-competitive activity and impose a fine accordingly. The Commission also publishes notices, which are not binding, specifying agreements which in its view do not fall within art.101(1) TFEU.

Negative clearance and comfort letters—now Guidance Letters

If an undertaking wishes to obtain official confirmation that an agreement is outside those prohibited by art.101(1) TFEU, it could seek negative clearance under Regulation 17/62. However, the Commission was spending a disproportionate amount of time in dealing with applications for negative clearance and applications for exemption under art.101(3) TFEU. When Regulation 1/2003 replaced Regulation 17/62 this situation was changed fundamentally. Under Regulation 1/2003 it was no longer necessary for the undertaking to notify the Commission in order to obtain negative clearance. The Regulation puts the burden on the undertaking to decide if it offends art.101 TFEU. To ease this workload and to speed up its decision-making processes, the Commission began to issue "comfort letters". These provided a quick and informal way of providing assurance for the parties concerned. A comfort letter is a communication from the Commission to the effect that, in its opinion, the agreement either does not infringe art.101(1) TFEU or that if it does infringe the article it is of a type that qualifies for exemption. The letter generally concludes with the statement that the Commission considers the "file closed". Such letters have been held by the Court to be outside the framework of Regulation 17/62 (now Regulation 1/2003) as they are only administrative letters and as such are not legally binding on national courts (see the *Perfumes* cases, Case 99/79 *SA Lancôme v Etos BV*). Also the Commission can reopen the file at any time. What the Commission can now do is to issue non-legally enforceable "guidance letters" under Regulation 1/2003.

All agreements or practices covered by art.81(1) EC (ex 85(1) EC) must be notified to the Commission as failure to do so, for any reason, may result in heavy fines being imposed by the Commission (see below, p.119).

Article 102 TFEU and the abuse of a dominant position

TREATY HIGHLIGHTER

ARTICLE 102 TFEU

Any abuse by one or more undertakings of a dominant position within the common market or in a substantial part of it shall be prohibited as incompatible with the common market in so far as it may affect trade between Member States. Such abuse may, in particular, consist in:

(a) directly or indirectly imposing unfair purchase or selling prices or unfair trading conditions;

(b) limiting production, markets or technical development to the prejudice of consumers;

(c) applying dissimilar conditions to equivalent transactions with other trading parties, thereby placing them at a competitive disadvantage; and

(d) making the conclusion of contracts subject to acceptance by the other parties of supplementary obligations which, by their nature or according to commercial usage, have no connection with the subject of such contracts.

There are three essential ingredients to this article. There must be a dominant position; an abuse of that position and that abuse must affect trade between the Member States.

Dominant Position   What is meant by dominance? The Court stated in Case 27/76 *United Brands v Commission* that it is "a position of economic strength enjoyed by an undertaking which enables it to prevent effective competition being maintained on the relevant market by giving it the power to behave to an appreciable extent independently of its competitors, customers and ultimately of its consumers".

KEY CASE

C-27/76 UNITED BRANDS V COMMISSION

Facts: United Brands was a company based in the USA which was the world's largest seller of bananas and owner of the Chiquita brand of bananas. As it handled 40% of the trade in bananas in the EU the Commission considered that it was in a dominant position in a substantial part of the Union. In addition to this large market share United Brands economic power was based upon the ownership of numerous plantations in tropical countries and a fleet of refrigerated banana boats plus controlling the 'ripeners' in EU countries. The European Commission reached the decision that United Brands was abusing its dominant position, contrary to art.102 **TFEU** (then art.86EC) and imposed a fine of 1m Euros. The company challenged the decision in an action for annulment under art.263 **TFEU** (then art.173 EC) on the basis that the Commission had looked at the wrong market to see if there was dominance—i.e. it should have been 'fruit' and not the 'banana' market.

Held: United Brands was partially successful in that the fine was reduced to 850,000 Euros and the Court said that the prices they charged were not excessive. However, the Court agreed that the appropriate market was the banana market.

Commentary: This case illustrates that it is not the dominance of a market by a company but the abuse of that economic power.. It also shows how the Commission has to research 'the market' to make sure that the Court is convinced that the appropriate market has been identified. This follows on from the problems that the Commission encountered in the *Continental Can* case (see below).

The Commission added in Case 62/86 *AKZO Chemie BV v Commission* "The power to exclude effective competition is not in all cases coterminous with independence from competitive factors but may also involve the ability to eliminate or seriously weaken existing competitors or to prevent potential competitors from entering the market". The existence of a dominant position is a question of fact determined by the relevant market factors. There has to be a relevant market for art.102 **TFEU** to operate, but this is not always easy to define. For example, in *United Brands* the Commission made a detailed analysis and concluded that the relevant market was the banana market, of which United Brands had a substantial share. The company argued that it was the fresh fruit market which was relevant, of which they had a much smaller share. The CJEU held that the banana market was in fact a distinct market because the characteristics of the consumers meant that the product was not interchangeable. In Case 6/72 *Europemballage and Continental Can v Commission* the problem of product substitution and the inability on the part of the Commission to define the relevant market led to the annulment of the Commission's Decision (see also Case 333/94 *Tetra-Pak International v Commission*).

With regard to the territory of the relevant market there is no fixed geographical definition. It could be a worldwide market or a narrowly localised market. The important point is that the abuse of the dominant position must take effect in the common market or a substantial part of it (Case 68/78 *Liptons Cash Registers v Hugin*). If there is an abuse of a dominant position under art.102 TFEU there is no exemption.

Enforcement of competition policy

The recent cases of C-95/04 *British Airways Plc v Commission* (extra commission payments for travel agents), T-340/03 *France Telecom SA v Commission* (predatory pricing) and T-201/04 *Microsoft Corp v Commission* (refusal to supply) demonstrate the vigilance of the Commission in policing arts 101 and 102 TFEU. The European Commission has a central role in enforcing the Community's competition policy through Directorate-General 4 (DG4), the department responsible. To fulfil its tasks the Commission enjoys substantial powers, subject to strict procedural requirements under Regulation 1/2003 and a general duty of confidentiality. A breach of these duties can result in the annulment of the Commission's Decision by the General Court and possibly a successful action for damages (Case 145/83 *Adams v Commission*).

Investigative powers

If the Commission is to undertake market analysis to enable it to make a Decision it needs powers of investigation.

(a) The Commission can request all information that is necessary to enable it to carry out its task from governments, competent authorities in the Member State such as the Office of Fair Trading in the UK, undertakings and associations of undertakings.

(b) The Commission may conduct general enquiries into whole sectors of the economy if economic trends suggest that competition in the common market is being restricted or distorted.

(c) The Commission may undertake all necessary on-the-spot investigations including entering premises, examining and copying business records and conducting oral examinations.

Before undertaking such investigations the officials of the Commission are required to produce written authorisation in the form of a Decision specifying the subject matter and purpose of the investigations (see Case 136/79 *National Panasonic v Commission* and Case 46/87 *Hoechst v Commission*). The undertakings are required to comply with the legitimate demands from the Commission. If they fail to do so or give false information they may be fined, as information cannot be withheld even if it is self-incriminating. In Case 155/79 *AM & S v Commission*, the CJEU stated that it was possible to claim privilege for correspondence between a client and an independent lawyer, but not where the lawyer is employed "in-house". This was confirmed in case C-550/07P *Akzo Nobel Chemicals* and *Akcros Chemicals v European Commission*, where the Court held that this applies even where the employed lawyer is a member of a national Bar.

KEY CASE

CASE C-550/07P AKZO NOBEL CHEMICALS LTD V COMMISSION

Facts: In February 2003 the Commission thought that Akzo Nobel Chemicals and its subsidiary Akcros Chemicals were involved in to possible anti-competitive practices and so ordered them to submit to an investigation aimed at seeking evidence. The investigation was carried out by Commission officials assisted by representatives of the Office of Fair Trading ('OFT', the British competition authority), at the applicants' premises in the United Kingdom.

During the examination of the documents seized a dispute arose in relation, in particular, to copies of two e-mails exchanged between the managing director and Akzo Nobel's coordinator for competition law, an Advocaat of the Netherlands Bar and a member of Akzo Nobel's legal department employed by that company. The Commission rejected the claim made by those two companies that the documents at issue should be covered by legal professional privilege. The companies challenged that view before the General Court and when this was dismissed they appealed to the CJEU.

Held: The Court dismissed the appeal because as a result of the in-house lawyer's economic dependence and the close ties with his employer, that he does not enjoy a level of professional independence comparable to that of an external lawyer. It followed that the General

Court did not commit an error of law with respect to the second condition for legal professional privilege laid down in the judgment in *AM& S Europe v Commission*.

Commentary: The Court identified the fundamental different position of the 'in-house' lawyer regardless of whether they were subject to the ethical obligations arising from being a member of a Bar or Law Society. The lack of independence is the important characteristic which such a lawyer does not share with the external lawyer.

Fines and penalties

The Commission has power under Regulation 1/2003 to impose fines for breaches of arts 101 and 102 TFEU. These can be up to one million Euros or 10 per cent of the undertaking's global turnover, whichever is the greater. The largest fine imposed to date has been that imposed by the Commission against those in the Vitamins Cartel in 2001 where a fine of over 855 million Euros was imposed. In 2002 The European Commission imposed fines totalling 478 million Euros on four companies which operated a long-running cartel on the market for plasterboard, a product which is widely used in the building industry and by DIY practitioners. Substantial fines have also been imposed on the US firm Microsoft. In 2014 the Commission imposed a fine of 953 million Euros on two European companies and four Japanese companies for operating a cartel in the market of automotive bearings. The agreement had operated for seven years and only came to the attention of the Commission when one Japanese company disclosed the information. That company escaped a fine as it benefited from the 2006 'Leniency Notice'.

None of the fine is paid to the party injured by the anti-competitive activity. Such victims must seek a remedy in their national courts. The size of the fine will depend on factors such as the nature and duration of the infringement, the economic importance of the undertakings and whether the parties have already infringed the Community's competition policy. The case law of the Court and Regulation 1/2003 confirm that a Commission decision is binding proof that the anti-competitive behaviour took place and was illegal. In June 2013 the Commission proposed a Directive that aims to make it easier for those affected by such behaviour to claim damages in their national courts.

Interim measures

Although not specifically granted under Regulation 1/2003, the Court has held that interim measures can be granted provided they were:

(1) indispensable,
(2) urgent, and

(3) necessary to avoid serious or irreparable damage to the party seeking the action or where there is a situation which is intolerable to the public interest (see Case 792/79 *Camera Care v Commission*).

Competition law and property rights

The CJEU has recognised that there has to be some protection given to owners of intellectual property rights such as patents or trademarks. If this were absent the incentive to advance technological developments would be removed. This is why art.36 TFEU provides derogation from art.34 TFEU, as discussed above. The Court has managed to balance these rights, confirmed in art.345 TFEU with the need not to impair competition. The specific subject matter of the right has been identified and protected but its exercise may be restricted or limited by the Treaty (see Joined Cases 56/64 and 58/64 *Consten and Grundig v Commission* (above) and Case 24/67 *Parke Davis v Centrafarm*). For example, the owner of a patent is entitled to his "reward" of a higher price when the goods are first put on the market. He cannot control their price or distribution by refusing parallel imports as this may affect trade between Member States.

However, the CJEU decision in Case 355/96 *Silhouette International v Hartlauer Hendelsgesellschaft* seemed to take a more restrictive view when interpreting the Trade Mark Directive 89/104. Silhouette was allowed to exercise its trademark rights to prevent the importation of its sunglasses from outside the EEA, where they had been sold at a lower price. The CJEU had decided that Silhouette's trademark rights had not been exhausted when they had sold the sunglasses to a retailer in Bulgaria and therefore outside the EEA. In the later case of Case 173/98 *Sebago Inc and Ancienne Maison Dubois et Fils SA v GB-UNIC SA* the CJEU confirmed its interpretation of the Directive, but did raise the possibility for the importer to show that the owner of the trademark had consented to the exhaustion of their rights. In the English case of *Zino Davidoff SA v A & G Imports Ltd* [2002] Ch. 109, where the facts concerned the importation of luxury perfumes, the trademark owner was held to have consented. The essential function of a trademark is to guarantee to consumers the real origin of goods or services, as the CJEU recently stated in the *Arsenal* case (Case 206/01 *Arsenal Football Club Plc v Reed*).

Anti-competitive behaviour by governments

Public undertakings and similar bodies are in principle subject to the same rules on competition as private undertakings (art.106 TFEU). However, they are exempted to the extent necessary to perform the particular tasks assigned to them. The Commission supervises such undertakings to ensure that the development of trade between the Member States is not affected.

With regard to state aids, art.107 TFEU prohibits any aid that distorts or threatens to distort competition by favouring certain undertakings or the production of certain goods. However, art.107(2) TFEU states that certain aid is always permissible, e.g. if it has a social character, and art.107(3) TFEU that other aids maybe permissible, e.g. for areas with high unemployment. There is a procedure laid down by art.108 TFEU by which the Commission can allow or prevent such aids.

EU merger policy

The Commission originally sought to deal with the impact of mergers on Community competition policy by using art.101 TFEU (Case 730/79 *Philip Morris v Commission*) and art.102 TFEU (Case C-6/72 *Continental Can above*). In September 1990 Council Regulation 4064/89, known as the Merger Regulation, came into force. This regulation applied to mergers involving enter- prises with an aggregate worldwide turnover of more than five billion Euros and where the aggregate Community turnover of each of at least two of the enterprises concerned is more than 250 million Euros. Even when these thresholds are not met the merger may still be covered by art.1(3) of Regulation 1310/97 where other turnover thresholds are specified. Such mergers are subject to examination by the European Commission, unless they are primarily within one Member State (see the *Aérospatiale–Alenia–de Haviland* case (Case IV/M53)). Regulation 1310/97 amended Regulation 4064/89 to facilitate greater procedural harmony in the assessment of different types of mergers.

Under art.2(3) of the Regulation there is a two-stage test of compatibility. The initial consideration is whether the concentration "creates or strengthens a dominant position within the common market or a substantial part of it". If this is satisfied, the Commission is required to assess whether the merger will significantly impede effective competition within the Community. The Commission will then either clear the merger, allowing it to take place, or stop it from taking place. This is not an easy task as is evidenced by the recent decisions by the General Court that annulled Commission decisions because the Court was not satisfied with the economic analysis of the anti-competition effects produced by the Commission. These were the cases of *Tetra Laval BV* (T-5/02) and Case T-77/02 *Schneider Electric SA v Commission*. Schneider subsequently brought a successful claim in damages against the Commission under art.340 TFEU in the case of T-351/03 *Schneider SA v Commission*.

The new Merger Regulation 139/2004 is the latest attempt by the Commission to improve the speed and efficiency of the control of "concentrations". This Regulation recognises that national controls may be more efficient if the EU is to compete in the global market. It provides for a "one-stop shop" so that clearance or refusal can be given quickly. The turnover thresholds under the new Regulation remain the same.

Remedies in the national courts

The courts of the Member States can apply arts 101 and 102 TFEU as they are directly effective. If the court applies the rule of reason devised by the CJEU to decide if the agreement is contrary to art.101(1) TFEU and comes to the conclusion that it does, it can only declare it void under art.101(2) TFEU. Only the Commission can grant exemption under art.101(3) TFEU and impose fines under Regulation 1/2003. The national court should grant the same remedies as would be available in similar actions under national law, including inter-locutory proceedings. However, in *Garden Cottage Foods Ltd v Milk Marketing Board* [1984] A.C. 130, the House of Lords left it unclear as to whether a breach of art.101 TFEU could give rise to a remedy in damages. In the sub-sequent case of C-453/99 *Courage Ltd v Crehan* the right for an individual to claim damages before a national court for breaches of arts 101 and 102 TFEU EC was recognised by the CJEU.

REVISION CHECKLIST

You should now know and understand:

☐ the role of competition policy in the EC

☐ the control of restrictive practices under art.101 TFEU

☐ the control of abuse of a dominant position under art.102 TFEU

☐ the role and powers of the European Commission in policing the competition policy

☐ the possibilities for exemption and negative clearance for businesses

☐ the enforcement of competition policy and Regulation 1/2003

☐ fines and penalties that can be imposed

☐ anti-competitive behaviour by governments

☐ the EU merger policy

☐ the remedies in the national courts

SUMMARY OF KEY CASES

Case	Court	Key Principle
C-145/83 Adams v Commission	CJEU	The CJEU has adopted a very restrictive interpretation of the tortuous liability of the Union— although Adams was successful.
Aerospatiale–Alenia–de Haviland case (Case IV/M53)	Commission Decision	Mergers are subject to examination by the Commission unless they are primarily within one member State.
C-62/86 AKZO Chemie BV v Commission	CJEU	AKZO in a dominant position cut its prices over a long period to put competitor our of business.
C-550/07P Akzo Nobel Chemicals and Akcros Chemicals v European Commission	CJEU	In-house lawyers are economically dependent on their employers so not in the same position as an external lawyer.
C-155/79 AM & S v Commission	CJEU	Possible to claim privilege for correspondence between a client and an independent lawyer.
C-206/01 Arsenal Football Club Plc v Reed	CJEU	The essential function of a trade mark is to guarantee to the consumer the real origin of the goods.
C-95/04 British Airways Plc v Commission	CJEU	The bonus schemes imposed by British Airways on travel agents that were conditional, individualised and retroactive were deemed to constitute an abuse of dominant position under art.102 TFEU.
C-792/79 Camera Care v Commission	CJEU	CJEU held that the Commission may grant interim relief in urgent cases where there is immediate danger of irreparable damage to the complainant.

123

Case	Court	Principle
C-56 & 58/64 Consten & Grundig v Commission	CJEU	Vertical as well as horizontal agreements could breach art.101 TFEU.
C-453/99 Courage Ltd v Crehan	CJEU	An individual can rely upon a breach of art.101(1) TFEU before a national court.
C-6/72 Europemballage and Continental Can v Commission	CJEU	Dominance in a market means 'power to behave independently without taking into account competitors, purchasers or suppliers...'.
T-340/03 France Telecom SA v Commission (predatory pricing)	General Court (then CFI)	F had engaged in predatory pricing— prices below average variable costs give grounds for assuming that a pricing practice is eliminatory and that, secondly, prices below average total costs but above average variable costs must be regarded as abusive if they are determined as part of a plan for eliminating a competitor.
Garden Cottage Foods Ltd v Milk Marketing Board [1984] A.C. 130,	House of Lords	Some doubt whether damages could be claimed for breach of art.101 TFEU —now no doubt they can—see Courage ltd v Crehan above.
C-46/87 Hoechst v Commission	CJEU	Commission entitled to undertake 'such investigations as are necessary'—including 'dawn raid'.
C-48/69 ICI v Commission (the Dyestuffs case)	CJEU	Irrelevant that there was no formal agreement because collusion could be identified.
C-68/78 Liptons Cash Registers v Hugin	Commission	Abuse of dominant position must take effect in the EU or a substantial part of it. C-22/78 Hugin v Commission.

T-201/04 Microsoft Corp v Commission	General Court	Microsoft had infringed art.102 TFEU by committing abuses of a dominant position (a) the refusal to supply its competitors and (b) by imposing linked transactions.
C-136/79 National Panasonic v Commission	CJEU	Commission must produce written authorisation in form of a Decision when undertaking investigations—Reg.1/2003.
C-24/67 Parke Davis v Centrafarm	CJEU	The exercise of patent rights cannot of itself fall either under art.101(1) TFEU, in the absence of any prohibited agreement, decision or concerted practice prohibited or under art.102 TFEU in the absence of any abuse of a dominant position.
C- 99/79 SA Lancôme v Etos (Perfumes cases)	CJEU	Comfort letters only had limited legal status as not 'decisions' they could not be challenged.
C-730/79 Philip Morris v Commission	CJEU	Art.101 TFEU originally used by Commission when dealing with mergers—now have Merger Regulation.
C-159/91 and 160/91 Poucet v AGF	CJEU	The Court distinguished between bodies pursuing economic activities and those without an intention of making a profit.
T-77/02 Schneider Electric SA v Commission	General Court (then the CFI)	According to the Commission the effects of the merger on competition affect all materials used for the distribution of electricity and the control of electric circuits at various levels (household, office, and factory). The Court challenged the Commission's economic analysis in support of its banning of the merger.

T-351/03 Schneider SA v Commission	General Court (then the CFI)	S successfully brought an action for damages against the Commission for the above case.
C-173/98 Sebago Inc and Ancienne Maison Dubois et Fils SA v GB-UNIC SA	CJEU	Possible for the importer to show that the owner of the trademark had consented to the exhaustion of their rights.
C-355/96 Silhouette International v Hartlauer Hendelsgesellschaft	CJEU	Owner of trademark rights had not exhausted their rights when selling outside the EEA.
C-333/94 Tetra-Pak International v Commission	CJEU	Tetra Pak group specialized in equipment for the packaging of liquid or semi-liquid food products in cartons. In 1983, 90% of cartons were used for the packaging of milk and other liquid dairy products. In 1987 that share was approximately 79%. TP argued that the Commission had not considered possible substitutes for their products.
T-5/02 Tetra Laval BV	General Court (then the CFI)	The Court agreed that the lack of horizontal, vertical and conglomerate anti-competitive effects well founded; the merger would not create a dominant position in the aseptic carton markets.
C-27/76 United Brands v Commission	CJEU	UB were dominant in the 'banana' market–distinct from the market for fresh fruit.

| Zino Davidoff SA v A & G Imports Ltd [2002] Ch. 109 & Joined Cases C-414/99 to C-416/99 | CJEU and High Court | The consent of a trade mark proprietor to the marketing within the EEA of products bearing that mark which have previously been placed on the market outside the EEA by that proprietor or with his consent may be implied but cannot be inferred from mere silence. |

QUESTION AND ANSWER

QUESTION

What powers are given to the European Commission with regard to the enforcement of EU competition policy?

ADVICE AND THE ANSWER

Introduction—the European Commission has been given extensive powers with regard to competition policy (art.101 TFEU) as they are seen to be the guardians of the Treaties (see art.17 TEU). The Treaties take the maintenance of competition very seriously and cover anti-competitive behaviour of undertakings or businesses (arts 101 & 102 TFEU) but also the governments of Member States (art.106 TFEU).

It is Regulation 1/2003, which replaced Regulation 17/62, which gives the Commission its investigative powers. These include the ability to undertake market analysis to enable it to make a Decision; it can request all information that is necessary to enable it to carry out its task from governments, competent authorities in the Member State, undertakings and associations of undertakings. It can conduct general enquiries into whole sectors of the economy if economic trends suggest that competition in the common market is being restricted or distorted. Finally, where necessary, the Commission may undertake all necessary on-the-spot investigations including entering premises, examining and copying business records and conducting oral examinations.

Only the European Commission can grant an exemption to undertakings where a breach of art.101(3) TFEU is concerned or can give approval to a Member State acting contrary to the principle of competition in special circumstances. The Commission can also impose fines of one million Euros or 10 per cent of the undertaking's global turnover whichever is the greater if there has been a breach of the competition rules. This demonstrates their authority in this area of policy. The Commission works closely with the national competition authorities but ultimately it is the Commission's responsibility to enforce the competition policy of the EU.

Free Movement of Workers

9

INTRODUCTION

The EU seeks to promote comprehensive economic integration and these provisions apply to all workers of the Member States, regardless of occupation. Since a common market requires the removal of all obstacles to the free movement of the factors of production, the free movement of workers in the Union may be seen as simply a prerequisite to the achievement of an economic objective. This chapter reviews the main points associated with the free movement of workers and their families.

The Treaties do not purport to establish an absolute freedom of migration in a general sense, but confine themselves to this economic activity. Eventually the object is to create a "common market in manpower", which would serve the purpose of moving labour to areas which reveal shortage of manpower and to solve the problem of unemployment in over-populated areas. Whether such a simplistic view can still be held in the light of future enlargement is an important question.

However this policy does not only have economic implications. There are also social consequences. The Preamble of Regulation 1612/68 (now amended by Directive 2004/38) stated:

> "The freedom of movement constitutes a fundamental right of
> workers and their families; mobility of labour within the Com-
> munity must be one of the means by which the worker is guar-
> anteed the possibility of improving his living and working con-
> ditions and promoting his social advancement, while helping to
> satisfy the requirements of the economy of the Member States".

The freedom of movement of workers is mainly based on the principle of non-discrimination on the ground of nationality, while the freedom of non- wage earners to move within the Union is, generally speaking, expressed by the right of establishment and the right to provide service. For the non-economically active three Directives were adopted in 1990 giving rights to those of independent means (Directive 90/364) and retired persons who did not satisfy Regulation 1251/70 (Directive 90/365). In addition there was Directive 90/366 which provided rights to students undertaking a vocational course at a university in another Member State whereby they can reside in the host Member State for the duration of their course. This Directive was later annulled by the Court (Case 295/90 *European Parliament v Council*) on the grounds that the legal base claimed by the Council was wrong so that the Parliament was merely consulted and the co-operation procedure was not utilised. However, the Directive remained in force until it was replaced by *Directive 93/96*. For all these directives there is one common factor, which is that the individual who is seeking to enforce a right under them is not economically dependent upon the benefits system of the host Member State. These directives are no longer in force because they have been superseded by a new Directive 2004/38 and more importantly by the development of the rights of "citizens of the EU". To try to show that the EU was not just for businesses and in an attempt to strengthen the links between the EU and its citizens, the concept of citizen of the EU was introduced in the Treaty of Maastricht and strengthened in the Treaty of Amsterdam. It is now stated in art.20 TFEU that every person holding the nationality of a Member State is a citizen of the Union. Importantly in the context of the free movement of workers is art.21 TFEU which states that every EU citizen has the right to move and reside freely within the territory of the Member States subject to any limitations and conditions laid down in the Treaties or by measures adopted to give them effect. The most important one of these conditions is that the citizen should not be a burden upon the welfare of the Member State. This condition has been tempered by CJEU judgments such as Case C-138/02 *Collins* where jobs seekers allowance was allowed to be claimed and Case C-209/03 *Bidar* where a subsidised student loan could be obtained. In C-333/13 *Dano* case the CJEU held that it was possible for the government of a Member State to refuse non-contributory benefits to a national from another Member State where they do not have the right of residence under Directive 2004/38. For example where they are not genuinely seeking employment.

Directive 2004/38, which came into force in May 2006, consolidates several provisions that affect the worker. It is known as the Citizens Free Movement Rights Directive and repealed Directive 68/360, arts 10 and 11 of Regulation 1612/68 and Directive 64/221.

Directives concerned determine the scope and detailed rules for exercise of rights conferred directly by the Treaty. No exit or entry visas are required from EU nationals, only an identity card or a passport.

C-127/08 Metock and Others v Minister of Justice, Equality and Law Reform

Facts: Four nationals of non-member countries had initially unsuccessfully applied for political asylum in Ireland and then married EU citizens who were not Irish nationals but who resided in Ireland. They had their applications for residence cards as spouses of Union citizens refused by the Minister for Justice on the ground that they did not satisfy the condition of prior lawful residence in another Member State laid down in Irish law. Those refusals formed the subject-matter of actions for annulment before the High Court which, after finding that none of the marriages in question was a marriage of convenience, referred to the Court of Justice questions for a preliminary ruling on the interpretation of **Directive 2004/38/EC** on the right of citizens of the Union and their family members to move and reside freely within the territory of the Member States in order to establish whether the Directive precludes legislation of a Member State which makes the right of residence of a national of a non-member country subject to the conditions of prior lawful residence in another Member States and acquisition of the status of spouse of a citizen of the Union before his/her arrival in the host Member State.

Held: The CJEU referred to several provisions **of Directive 2004/38/EC,** as well as on its earlier case-law concerning the free movement of persons, the Court determined that the Directive does not make its application conditional on the beneficiaries, family members of a citizen of the Union, having previously resided in a Member State. Finally, the Court stated that the provisions of the Directive should be interpreted in a non-restrictive way.

Commentary: In reaching its judgment the Court reversed its findings in Case C-109/01 *Akrich* where it had accepted that Member States could impose national conditions.

Concept of "worker"

Article 45 TFEU refers to "freedom of movement for workers" and art.1 of Regulation 1612/68 on Freedom of Movement for Workers within the Community referred to the right to "take up an activity as an employed person", but neither give definitions. The Court has said that the words must be given their ordinary meaning and not interpreted restrictively. However, the concept only covers pursuit of effective and genuine activities. Provided that he pursues this effective and genuine activity the motives of the individual are not to be taken into account. In Case 66/85 *Lawrie-Blum v Land Baden-Württemberg* the CJEU suggested that the essential characteristics of a worker are of someone who performs services for another during a certain period of time and under the direction of another in return for remuneration. In the *Levin* case (Case 53/81) the Court held that those who worked part-time were included provided the work was "real" work and not nominal or minimal (see Case 139/85 *Kempf v Staatssecretaris van Justitie*).

Regulation 1408/71 (now replaced by Regulation 883/2004) defines a worker as anyone who is insured either compulsorily or voluntarily within the framework of a social security system of a Member State organised for the benefit of salaried employees.

The definition of "worker" in the Union sense rarely causes difficulty because if an economically active claimant under art.45 TFEU is not a worker, he is probably self-employed in which case art.49 or 56 TFEU would apply. The CJEU has held that arts 45, 49 and 56 TFEU are based on the same principles as far as entry, residence and non-discrimination on the grounds of nationality are concerned and so categorisation under art.45, as opposed to art.49 or 50 TFEU will rarely be crucial. This is even more so since the increase in the rights of the EU citizen mentioned above and detailed in arts 18 to 25 TFEU.

Removal of restrictions

The Council issued Directive 68/360 on the abolition of restrictions on movements and residence for workers of the Member State and their families. Both art.45 TFEU and the Directive have been held by the CJEU to be directly effective, giving individuals' rights that the courts in the Member States must protect and enforce. Directive 2004/38 has replaced Directive 68/360.

Article 45(3) TFEU envisages the free movement of workers for pursuit of accepting employment but makes no mention of a right to move freely in search of employment. Directive 68/360 made no reference to this point either, but it has been generously interpreted by the Court. In Case 48/75 *Procureur du Roi v Royer* the Court held that art.3 of the Directive included the right of workers to enter the territory of a Member State and reside there for the purposes intended by the Treaty, in particular to look for or pursue an activity as an employed person. In the *Levin* case this right was limited to three months on the proviso that the individual could support themselves without recourse to public assistance. Also in Case 292/89 *R. v Immigration Appeal Tribunal, Ex p. Antonissen* the Court held that immigrants seeking employment had the right to enter another Member State and stay there for a sufficient period of time to find out about the job market opportunities and to find a job. In the UK six months is allowed for a "worker" to find a job although generally at least three months are given by Member States.

Right of residence

A worker's right to a residence permit is implied once he has secured a job but if he finds no job or if he loses it voluntarily he cannot expect to be entitled to a residence permit. Thus a British subject continuously unemployed was not entitled to a renewal of his residence permit in the Netherlands—*Williams v Dutch Secretary of State* (1977).

The right of residence means the right to stay indefinitely in the host country. A worker cannot be expelled except in cases justifiable under derogation from the freedom of movement (see Limitations below, p.136). The residence permit is issued for a period of five years but it is renewable. The permit is merely proof of the right granted by the Treaty that exists independently of the document.

Directive 2004/38

Articles 16–18 of this Directive replace Regulation 1251/70. As a corollary to the freedom of movement protected by Regulation 1612/68 and Directive 68/360, Regulation 1251/70 (now Directive 2004/38) gave the worker the right to remain in the territory of a Member State after having been employed there. This right applies to the retired and the incapacitated worker. A worker acquires a right of residence on retirement provided that he has reached the age laid down in that Member State for entitlement to an old-age pension, and has resided continuously in that Member State for more than three years the last year of which he has been employed. If the incapacity of the worker is due to an industrial accident or disease entitling him to the payment of a pension, he can remain in the Member State regardless of the length of his previous residence. If the incapacity did not arise from employment he is entitled to remain if he has resided in the Member State for at least two years.

Worker's dependants

The principle of non-discrimination must be extended to his or her dependants; otherwise the practical implementation becomes meaningless. This non-discrimination as regards dependants must not be limited to the right to reside in another Member State, together with the worker. It must encompass the whole treatment afforded to national dependants, including education, training, welfare and housing.

Under art.2 of Directive 2004/38 family members include not only the spouse but also a partner in a registered partnership.

In principle members of the family have rights analogous to the rights of the person primarily concerned, i.e. entry, residence and exit, together with social security rights. Family rights terminate with the primary rights of the worker and also when a dependant ceases to be a member of the family, e.g. divorced spouse or a married child).

Directive 2004/38 would now cover this situation and so the individual would no longer be dependent upon the law in any one Member State.

KEY CASE

CASE 59/85 NETHERLANDS STATE V REED

Facts: Miss Reed, an unmarried British national, arrived in the Netherlands in November 1981 and registered for employment but she did not succeed in finding a job. In March 1982 she applied for a residence permit on the ground that she was living with Mr W. Mr W, who was also an unmarried British national, had worked in the Netherlands and had obtained a residence permit as a national of a Member State of the EU. On the date of the contested decision Miss Reed and Mr W. were living together in the Netherlands and had a stable relationship of some five years standing. The right of a 'spouse' was specified in art.10 of **Regulation 1612/68** (now **Directive 2004/58**) but that referred to a marital relationship. As a consequence the Netherlands said that she had no right of residence.

Held: the Court ruled that an interpretation of 'spouse' must take into consideration the situation within the whole Union, not just in one State. Furthermore the Court stated that the right to be accompanied by an unmarried companion is a social advantage and governed by the principle of non-discrimination. It followed that a Member State cannot grant an advantage to its own nationals and refuse it to other EU workers based on their nationality.

Commentary: Exercising its powers of interpretation the Court looked at the purpose of the EU legislation and pointed to the fact that under Dutch law the rights of a cohabitee were recognized so that meant that Reed could not be discriminated against in the same circumstances. **Directive 2004/58** now includes cohabiting couples (see art.2(2)(b)).

The death of the holder of primary rights will not deprive members of his family of their right to remain in the country. If not already acquired the workers survivors will do so if:

(a) resided continuously in the host country for two years preceding his death; or

(b) the worker died from an occupational disease or an industrial accident; or

(c) the surviving spouse was a national of the host country and lost that nationality on marriage to him.

Freedom of movement could nevertheless be illusory if by moving from one Member State to another the worker would lose the rights acquired under social security regulations, notably with regards to the pension rights of the worker and his dependants. The divorce or annulment of marriage or civil partnership may not affect the right of residence of a non-EU national (see *Baumbast and R.* [2004]).

The Treaty has therefore provided for the adoption of a system ensuring that:

(a) all periods are taken into account under the laws of the several countries where the beneficiary has worked will be added together for calculating the amount of his benefits; and

(b) that those benefits will be paid to the beneficiary in whichever Member State he resides.

Overall, therefore, the freedom of movement for the worker means applying the same treatment to the migrant worker and dependants as to the nationals of the Member State of residence.

LEGISLATION HIGHLIGHTER

Obstacles to the Free Movement of Workers

1. Discrimination based on nationality.
2. Incompatibility of the various social security systems.
3. Recognition of educational/professional qualifications.

Therefore any discrimination based on nationality between workers of the Member States as regards employment, remuneration and other labour conditions must be abolished. The workers' rights include:

(a) to accept offers of employment actually made;

(b) to move freely within the territory of a Member State for this purpose;

(c) to enter into and reside in a Member State for the purpose of employment in accordance with the provisions governing the employment of nationals of that Member State laid down by law, regulation or administrative action; and

(d) to remain in the territory of a Member State after having been employed in that state.

Public service employment

The principle of non-discrimination does not apply to employment in the public service art.45(4) states, which means that public authorities may refuse to hire non-nationals, but they have to justify such exclusion (Case 137/80 *Commission v Belgium*). The Court has held that the exemption provided by art.45(4) TFEU does not apply to all employment in the public sector as this is too wide an interpretation. Article 45(4) TFEU applies to those activities in the public service which were connected with the exercise of discretion or official authority involving the national interest. However, once a worker from another Member State is employed in the public service, he must be treated in the same way as the nationals, since exception only concerns access to the post (Case 152/73 *Sotgiu v Deutsche Bundespost*).

Limitations to the free movement of workers

The limitations specified in art.45(3) TFEU are on the grounds of Public Policy, Public Security or Public Health. National authorities applying these provisions upon an EU national must justify their action. They cannot impose restrictions upon a Union national unless "his presence or conduct constitutes a genuine and sufficiently serious threat to public policy"—see Case 36/75 *Roland Rutili v Ministre de l'interieur*. This cannot be applied to a group, but only to individual members of the group (see Case 41/ 74 *Van Duyn v Home Office*). On the basis of the UK government's view of the Church of Scientology, the Court held in *Van Duyn* that the UK's action was justified. The question was asked "Was it discriminatory in that a UK national could have taken up the post Van Duyn had accepted?" The Court response was:

> " ... a Member State for reasons of public policy, can where it deems necessary, refuse a national of another Member State the benefit of the principle of freedom of movement of workers in a case where such a national proposes to take up a particular offer of employment even though the Member State does not place a similar restriction on its own nationals".

It follows from the case law of the Court that Member States have not relinquished all control over Community nationals as regulations governing the registration of aliens and criminal sanctions in this respect are compatible with their Treaty obligations unless they are so rigorous as to be tantamount to a denial of the freedom of movement over and above the cases covered by the derogation provisions.

Public Policy provides a Member State with discretion but only within the limits allowed for by the Treaty, which are narrowly interpreted by the CJEU. Criminal conviction does not automatically justify deportation (see Case

67/74 *Bonsignore v Stadt Köln*). In Case 30/77 *R. v Bouchereau* a conviction for drug offences was regarded as a sufficient ground for deportation.

KEY CASE

CASE C-67/74 BONSIGNORE V STADT KÖLN

Facts: Bonsignore was an Italian national residing in Germany. The local German criminal court found him guilty of possession of a firearm and imposed a fine for breach of the firearms legislation. The court also found him guilty of causing death of his brother by negligence, but imposed no penalty on this count, considering that no purpose would be served in the circumstances, notably the mental suffering caused by the death of his brother. Following this criminal conviction the German authorities ordered that he be deported as a general preventive measure, as an example to others who may also be in illegal possession of firearms. Bonsignore appealed against this decision, during which a reference was made to the European Court under art.267 **TFEU** (then art.177 **EC**).

Held: Bonsignore had rights under EU law and specifically **Directive 64/221** (see now art.28 **Directive 2004/38**) and before any deportation on the grounds of public policy. Any action taken on the grounds of public policy must be based exclusively on the personal conduct of the individual concerned. Therefore Bonsignore's deportation was against EU law.

Commentary: In subsequent cases the Court stated that the Member State should take into consideration a number of factors before making an expulsion on grounds of public policy. These included how long the individual had been in residence, his age, stated health, family and economic situation, and integration into the host Member State.

REVISION CHECKLIST

You should now know and understand:

☐ the definition of "a worker"

☐ the Treaty provisions—arts 45, 46 & 48 TFEU

☐ the protection provided by Regulation 1612/68 and Directive 68/360, Directive 2004/38

☐ the special rules for public service employment

☐ the limitations to the free movement of workers

☐ the derogation provisions

FREE MOVEMENT OF WORKERS

SUMMARY OF KEY CASES

Case	Court	Key Principle
C 413/99 Baumbast and R.	CJEU	The primary carer of children irrespective of his nationality has right to reside with them in order to facilitate the exercise of that right notwithstanding the fact that the parents have meanwhile divorced.
C-209/03 Bidar	CJEU	As a French national resident in the UK for three years B must not be discriminated against when applying for a student loan.
C- 67/ 74 Bonsignore v Oberstadtdirektor der Stadt Köln	CJEU	Public policy or security cannot be justified on grounds extraneous to the individual.
C-138/02 Collins	CJEU	Concept of 'citizenship' introduced in the TEU meant that work-seeker could claim entitlement to benefits.
C-137/80 Commission v Belgium	CJEU	States have to justify where they discriminate in the appointment of public officers.
C-333/13 Dano v Jobcentre Leipzig	CJEU	Member States can refuse non-contributory benefits to nationals of other Member States where they do not have a right of residence under Dir.2004/38.
C-295/90 European Parliament v Council	CJEU	CJEU upheld the challenge of the EP and ordered that the Directive be annulled and new measure proposed.
C-139/85 Kempf v Staatssecretaris van Justitie	CJEU	Part-time work if it was 'real work' could recognise the person as a 'worker'.

C-66/85 Lawrie-Blum v Land Baden-Württemberg	CJEU	Even if the remuneration is minimal a person can still qualify as a worker.
C-53/81 Levin case	CJEU	Those who work part-time are 'workers' work.
C-127/08 Metock and Others v Minister of Justice, Equality and Law Reform	CJEU	National legislation cannot require the third-country-national spouse of an EEA citizen who is exercising his or her free movement rights in a host Member State to have been previously lawfully resident in another Member State before they can benefit from the provisions of the Free Movement Directive.
C-59/85 Netherlands State v Reed	CJEU	If a Member State does not discriminate between its own married and cohabiting couples then it cannot do so for partners from elsewhere in the EEA.
C-292/89 R. v Immigration Appeal Tribunal, Ex p. Antonissen	CJEU	Work-seekers do have certain rights but these were not indefinite. The six month limit was not insufficient to look for work.
C-36/75 Roland Rutili v Ministre de l'interieur	CJEU	The government must give a precise and comprehensive statement of the reasons for its decision.
C-152/73 Sotgiu v Deutsche Bundespost	CJEU	Indirect discrimination meant that the German nationals were more likely to qualify for the higher allowance.

C-41/74 Van Duyn v Home Office	CJEU	'It would be incompatible with the binding effect attributed to a Directive.. to exclude, in principle, the possibility that the obligation which is imposes may be invoked by those concerned.'
Williams v Dutch Secretary of State (1977) 1 CMLR 669	Afdeling Rechtspraak van de Raad van State (NL)	An individual who cannot find work or who voluntarily relinquishes a job is not entitled to be issued with or have a residence permit renewed.

QUESTION AND ANSWER

QUESTION

Advise Thomas, a German national on the following circumstances:
(a) having been employed as a part-time computer programmer in the UK for the past 16 months Thomas receives a letter from the UK authorities stating that he has 28 days in which to find full-time employment or else he must leave the country as he is unable to support himself;
(b) as a result of the economic situation in the UK Thomas decides to go to France. However, he is refused entry at Calais because he is a prominent member of the Animal Life Front, a group dedicated to the idea of protecting animals from slaughter for food products. It appears that the French authorities are afraid that his presence will cause violent demonstrations by France's farming lobby;
(c) Thomas is ultimately offered a full-time post in Spain. The Spanish authorities issue him with a residence permit but stipulate that his American wife can only visit him for a maximum period of four weeks every three months.

ADVICE AND THE ANSWER

Introduction—this problem question involves the rights given to an individual to move freely within the EU as a worker. Article 45 TFEU gives an individual who is a worker in one Member State the freedom to move to another Member State to accept offers of employment actually made. There is no definition of worker in the Treaty but subsequent secondary legislation and case law has provided such a definition (*Lawrie-Blum* case).

(a) It was held in *Levin* (1982) that the term worker and the associated rights applied to those who worked part-time as well as full-time provided that the work was "real" work and not minimal or minimal (*Kempf* (1986)). It would seem that the UK authorities are acting contrary to EU law. However, it is recognised that it is important that someone claiming the right of free movement should not become a burden on the social security system of the host Member State.

(b) Article 45 TFEU allows for derogation whereby the Member State does not have to fulfil their obligations under the Treaties. This includes the public policy ground but this has been interpreted very restrictively by the CJEU (*Van Duyn* case (1975)) and cannot be determined by the Member State without regard to EU policy (*Rutili* (1976)). Article 3(1) of **Directive 64/221** states that where this ground is used it must be based exclusively on the personal conduct of the individual. Would this include membership of the Animal Life Front? Also under art.6 of the Directive Thomas is entitled to know the ground for the refusal and this will help him prepare for any legal action.

(c) Article 10(1) of **Regulation 1612/68** defines those who may install themselves with the worker in the host Member State and this includes the worker's spouse, irrespective of her nationality. So Thomas's wife should be able to live with him all the time he is exercising his rights as a worker in Spain.

The Freedom of Establishment and the Freedom to Provide Services

10

FREEDOM OF ESTABLISHMENT

INTRODUCTION

As the initial emphasis of the EU was to exploit economic activity there was a need to facilitate the freedom of movement of professionals and companies. This chapter reviews the law as it applies to those exercising these freedoms.

Articles 49–55 TFEU

The right of establishment, necessary to exercise a profession or to render a service, is not confined to individuals. It is available to companies and bodies corporate which are treated like individuals. The immigration rules are broadly like those that apply to "workers", but the full enjoyment of "the right of establishment" depends upon the recognition of professional qua-lifications and this, in turn, depends upon the progress of harmonisation of national laws in this field.

There is no definition of the group of persons entitled to the right of establishment. In distinction from "workers" (who are salaried) art.49 TFEU contemplates a group of people who, in principle, pursue activities as self-employed persons or set up and manage undertakings within the meaning of art.54 TFEU.

Such persons belong, as a rule, to recognised professions whose status and membership is regulated by law. Hence the need of harmonising the national rules and regulations to facilitate their mobility within the Union and, in the first place, to remove restrictions on the ground of nationality and other peculiar national grounds (see Case 213/89 *R. v Secretary of State for Transport, Ex p. Factortame*).

To carry out its mandate the Council adopted in 1962 two General Programmes for the:

(i)   Abolition of Restrictions on Freedom to provide Services; and

(ii) on Freedom of Establishments;

and in subsequent years has embarked on extensive legislation in these fields. However, as the Commission recorded in its White Paper on completing the internal market, the results as of 1987 were still unsatisfactory. Therefore the Commission recommended action in specific areas including a more efficient policing and enforcement system, resulting in measures to suspend the enforcement of any national legislation which manifestly infringes EU law.

Independently of this harmonisation policy, the CJEU was able to remove some of the restrictions in accordance with the principle of non-discrimination. Thus it has held that a Dutch national resident in Belgium with the appropriate qualifications to practice law could not be debarred from his professional activity on the ground that, according to Belgian law, a lawyer must be a Belgian national (Case 2/74 *Reyners v Belgian State*). Similarly the Court ruled in the case of a Belgian lawyer (Case 71/76 *Thieffry v Conseil de l'Ordre des Avocats á la Cour de Paris*), a British architect qualified to practise in France (Case 11/77 *Patrick v Ministe're des Affaires Culturelles*) and a Dutch motor insurance claims investigator in Italy (Case 90/76 *Van Ameyde v UCI*).

The principle of non-discrimination on the ground of nationality was further extended when the Court held that residential qualification of a properly qualified person was not a legitimate condition of his exercising the profession.

However, conviction for the illegal exercise of the veterinary profession was upheld in the case of a person qualified in Italy who, having become naturalised in France, attempted to practise on his own without first obtaining the requisite French qualifications. (Case 136/78 *Ministère Public v Auer*) Such a bar was considered justified pending the implementation of the harmonising directives but no longer after. In the recent Case 55/94 *Reinhard Gebhard v Consiglio dell'Ordine degli Avvocati e Procuratori di Milano*, the CJEU brought the rules relating to establishment into line with those relating to services.

KEY CASE

CASE 55/94 REINHARD GEBHARD V CONSIGLIO DELL'ORDINE DEGLI AVVOCATI E PROCURATORI DI MILANO

Gebhard was a German national and a member of Stuttgart Bar. He had resided in Milan since 1978 and initially operated as an associate at a set of chambers there advising clients on aspects of German law. In 1989 he opened his own chambers and began to use the title 'avvocato' on his letterhead. Following complaints from some Italian practitioners to the Milan Bar Council he was banned from establishing his chambers. He could carry out professional activities on a temporary basis as a lawyer qualified in another Member State but not set up on a permanent basis. Gebhard argued that **Directive 77/249** (see below) entitled him to pursue his professional activities from his own chambers in Milan.

Held: The Court decided that given the time that Gebhard had been in Milan he had gone beyond merely providing services and had become established there. As such the Directive did not apply but he could rely on arts 43 & 49 **EC** (now arts 49 & 56 **TFEU**).

Commentary: In this judgment the Court reiterated that 'establishment' was the right of a Union national to participate on a stable and continuous basis in the economic life in a Member State and the 'provision of services' was of a temporary or discontinuous nature. It went on to say that any national measures that hinder or made less attractive such activities must fulfil four conditions—be applied in a non-discriminatory manner; must be justified in terms of meeting some imperative requirement in the public interest; be suitable to achieve this objective and must not go beyond what was necessary to achieve this aim, i.e. proportional. The judgment in this case confirmed the approach the Court had taken in the case C-76/90 *Manfred Säger v Dennemeyer & Co. Ltd*, which involved a patent agent.

"economic activities".   Amateur activities seem unaffected by EU rules. In Case 415/93 *Bosman* the CJEU held that arts 45 and 56 TFEU can in certain circumstances impose obligations on individual football clubs and associations not to impose restrictions on the free movement of footballers. In other words the sports organisations must comply with Union law in so far as sport constituted an 'economic activity'. The Court has had to apply these rules in a recent case involving judo. In Joined cases C-51/96 and C-191/97 *Christelle Deliège v Ligue Francophone de Judo et Disciplines ASBL* (the *Deliège* case) the matter before the Court was a dispute in Belgian over the rules limiting the selection of competitors for international competitions in judo. Deliège thought that her career was being frustrated when she was not being selected to compete for Belgium. The Court held that national federations are entitled to lay down their own rules when selecting national representatives.

FREEDOM TO PROVIDE SERVICES

Articles 56–62 TFEU

According to art.56 TFEU services mean "services for remuneration in particular activities of an industrial and commercial character, craftsmanship and exercise of a profession". However, the provision of services is often connected with the exercise of a profession and in this respect inseparable from the right of establishment. The difference between the provision of services and that of establishment is that the latter is associated with actually setting up in another Member State whereas the former involves only a transient visit to provide the services. Directive 2006/123 covers both the right to provide services and the right of establishment.

Right to receive services

Although arts 56 and 57 TFEU provide for the removal of restrictions on the freedom to provide services on the basis of Directive 73/148, they have been interpreted by the European Court of Justice to embrace the freedom to receive services. In Joined Cases 286/82 and 26/83 *Luisi v Ministero del Tesoro*, following the Commission's view in Case 118/75 *Criminal Proceedings against Watson and Belman*, the Court held that there was a freedom for the recipient of services to go to another Member State, without restriction, in order to receive a service there. Although the case involved the transfer of money out of Italy in breach of Italian currency law for the purpose of tourism and medical treatment, the principle in the judgment included persons travelling for the purpose of education. The right of residence exists during the period for which the service is provided. Any breach of this freedom would be prima facie a breach of arts 56 and 57 TFEU (see *R. v Secretary of State for the Home Department, Ex p. Flynn* [1997] 3 C.M.L.R. 888). Directive 2004/38 deals specifically with the situation where a student moves to another Member State to undertake a vocational course.

The student, spouse and dependent children have the right to remain for the duration of the course. In every case the student must assure the relevant national authority that he has sufficient resources to avoid becoming a burden on the social assistance system of the host Member State during the period of residence. In *Watts v Bedford Primary Care Trust* (2003) the right to go to another Member State to receive medical treatment at the expense of the NHS was upheld.

Vocational training

The Court has given a wide definition to the meaning of vocational education. In Case 293/83 *Gravier v City of Liège* the Court held it to include all forms of teaching which prepares for and leads directly to a particular profession or which provides the necessary skills for such a profession. In these circumstances a student may claim equal access and on the same basis as nationals of the Member State. This was confirmed in Case 24/86 *Blaizot v University of Liège*, where the course involved was a university veterinary studies course.

Derogation

As with all the freedoms arising from the Treaty there are exceptions where the Member State may derogate from their obligation under the Treaty. These are specifically those in arts 52 and 62 TFEU, which allow for derogation on the grounds of public policy, public security and public health. The public policy provision has been interpreted strictly by the European Court to ensure that its scope is not unilaterally determined by a Member State without control by the European Community institutions (*Van Duyn*). In Case 36/75 *Rutili v Ministre de l'Interieur* the Court held that restrictions on the movement of an EU national on the grounds of public policy could only be accepted where the behaviour of the individual constitutes a genuine and sufficiently serious threat to public policy.

Directive 2004/38

Article 27(2) of Directive 2004/38 states that any exclusion on the grounds of public policy or public security must be based exclusively on the personal conduct of the individual. In *Van Duyn* the Court held that although past association with an organisation does not count as personal conduct, present association does and the activities in question must constitute a genuine and sufficiently serious threat to public policy affecting one of the fundamental interests of society. In this case the Court allowed the UK to apply a stricter standard on an EU national than the one it applied to its own nationals because the UK deemed that it was necessary. In *Bonsignore* it was accepted that the concept of personal conduct expresses the requirement that a deportation order may only be made for breaches of the peace and public security that might be committed by the individual concerned.

Under art.30 of Directive 2004/38 the individual is entitled to know on which ground, i.e. public policy or public security, the decision is based, unless this information contravenes state security. This allows the individual to prepare his defence. If a Member State fails to comply with art.6 it may lead to the quashing of a deportation order (see *R. v Secretary of State for the Home Office, Ex p. Dannemberg* [1984] Q.B. 766). Article 8 of the Directive requires that the individual is entitled to the same legal remedies in relation to a decision on entry as any other national. For example in the UK an immigrant normally has a right of appeal against immigration decisions to a person called an adjudicator and then to the Immigration Appeal Tribunal.

Such appeals cover issues of fact, law and the exercise of discretion, so the merits of the decision would be fully reviewed. See also case C-60/00 *Mary Carpenter v SS for the Home Dept* where the spouse of a UK national providing services in a number of Member States was able to reside in the UK.

Mutual recognition

The European Community principle of equal treatment is not always sufficient to ensure that the immigrant is able to practice his profession in another Member State. There is no directly applicable provision in the EU Treaty requiring Member States to recognise qualifications acquired in another Member State or obliging them to allow immigrants to practice a profession without the appropriate qualifications (Case 136/78 *Ministère Public v Auer*). In order to make the right of establishment effective the Union embarked on a harmonising process in which the rules governing the formation and exercise of the medical profession took the lead. Article 53 TFEU requires the European Parliament and the Council to adopt directives on the mutual recognition of diplomas, certificates and other evidence of formal qualifications. Without a relevant directive the migrant is likely to find that Union law is of limited assistance to him. The Commission had attempted to remedy the situation by promoting separate directives for each profession, such as medicine, dentistry, veterinary medicine, midwifery and the exercise of the profession of architect. The objective of these directives has been to make it easier for a person practising a profession in one Member State to practice that profession in another Member State.

However, in order to avoid legislating piecemeal the Mutual Recognition Directive 89/48 was adopted. Like all directives on establishment Directive 89/48 benefits Union citizens with regard to qualifications awarded in a Member State. Directive 2005/36 replaced this earlier Directive and retained the essential content as a way forward. Under this Directive recognition is to be given to diplomas as defined by art.1. There must be three essential characteristics for such "diplomas"; it must be awarded by a competent authority in a Member State following the successful completion of a course lasting at least three years at a university or equivalent institution plus professional training. Finally, such a "diploma" must qualify the holder for the pursuit of a regulated profession in a Member State. Article 3 of the Directive provides the basic rule that if a Member State requires a "diploma" as a condition for exercising a regulated profession, it must accept a "diploma" obtained in another Member State.

Lawyers

The Commission had attempted to deal with various professional bodies by promoting separate directives for each. The objective of these directives has been to make it easier for a person practising a profession in one Member State to practice that profession in another Member State. However, the important difference between these professions and lawyers is that although the principles of medicine or dentistry are much the same in every Member State, those of law differ. It is therefore hardly surprising that the progress on facilitating the free movement of lawyers has been very slow.

Directive 77/249 (the Services Directive) was specifically aimed at lawyers but it is only concerned with the provision of services and not the right of establishment, which was dealt with by the Lawyer's Establishment Directive 98/5. It makes provision for lawyers to carry out their profession in another Member State on a temporary basis. (See *Reinhard Gebhard* case above). "Lawyer" under this Directive is defined by a list of terms to reflect the diversity in the European Union. The function of the list is to indicate those practitioners who are able to benefit from the rights conferred by the Directive and the activities to which it applies. Thus anyone who is recognised as a "lawyer" for the purpose of the Directive can perform the work of a lawyer in another Member State but only on a temporary basis. While he is performing this work he must use the title of his home country, as it would appear in that country. In this capacity the foreign lawyer can do all the work of a local lawyer, unless the national law of the Member State reserves certain activities for its national lawyers and on the proviso that he represents a client in court work in conjunction with a local lawyer. In the UK such foreign lawyers cannot undertake probate or conveyance work, which is reserved for UK lawyers. The Lawyers' Establishment Directive 98/5 confers rights on lawyers qualified in one Member State to practice in another.

The Mutual Recognition Directive 2005/36 discussed above applies to the legal profession. The profession of a lawyer is in the list of regulated professions. Article 3 of the Directive provides the basic rule that if a Member State requires a "diploma" as a condition for exercising a regulated profession, it must accept a "diploma" obtained in another Member State. In contrast to the situation where a lawyer is providing a "service" of a temporary nature, when he is exercising the right of establishment the lawyer is entitled to use the professional designation of the Member State in which he practices. Thus a French avocat who establishes himself and practices in the UK can call himself a solicitor.

The Directive recognises that professional training does vary between Member States and allows the Member State where the individual wishes to practice to set certain conditions. This may involve an adaptation period during which supervision by a qualified practitioner is required of the foreign national or an aptitude test of professional knowledge. In England the test for foreign lawyers wishing to practice as solicitors is called the Qualified Lawyers Transfer Test (now covered by the Qualified Lawyers Transfers Scheme

Regulations 2011). Having successfully passed this test the normal rules concerning registration and admission to the appropriate professional body will apply. In Case 313/01 *Morgenbesser* [2004] the Italian Bar refused to recognise as equivalent university study by the student in France as that undertaken by an Italian law student. The CJEU agreed with the Italian Bar.

Companies

The EU Treaty identified two rights for companies, namely establishment and provision of services and these are now embedded within the Treaty of Lisbon. Under art.49 TFEU companies have the right to establish themselves in another Member State by setting up agencies, branches or subsidiaries. Having so established themselves, the companies have the right not to be discriminated against and must be treated under the same conditions as those laid down by the Member State for its own nationals. The same rule applies to companies as it does to individuals, who must be nationals of a Member State if they are to benefit from the freedom specified in the Treaty. Article 54(1) TFEU specifies that as far as companies are concerned they must be formed in accordance with the law of a Member State and have their registered office, central administration or principal place of business within the Community. The Court of Justice held in Case 79/85 *Segers* that to allow a Member State in which a company carried on its business to treat that company in a different manner solely because its registered office was in another Member State would render art.54 TFEU valueless. This was confirmed by the CJEU in Case 212/97 *Centros Ltd*, which involved an attempt by the Danish Trade and Companies Board to refuse to register a company set up, but not trading, in England.

KEY CASE

C-212/97 CENTROS LTD

Facts: B was a Danish national who came to the UK in May 1992 to register her company, Centros. Under UK company law there is no specified paid up capital in order to benefit from limited liability. Following registration of her company B requested the Danish Trade and Companies Board to register a branch of Centros in Denmark. They refused on the basis that the company had never traded and that B was seeking to use the company to circumvent the Danish law requiring a minimum of 200,000 Danish Krona of capital. B challenged the decision of the Board in the Danish court and a reference was made to the CJEU.

Held: The CJEU stated that the refusal by the Trade and Companies

Board was contrary to arts 43 and 49 EC (now arts 49 & 56 TFEU). Centros was a company formed in accordance with the legal requirements of one Member State (the UK) and had to be recognised as such by the government of another Member State (namely Denmark).

Commentary: The CJEU is confirming its literal approach towards the freedom of establishment articles in the Treaties. This approach was followed in the similar case of C-167/01 *Inspire Art Ltd* involving registration of a branch in the Netherlands.

Just as there is a requirement that workers and the self-employed should receive remuneration in order to satisfy the Treaty, so companies which are non-profit making do not come within the definition of art.54(1) TFEU. The remuneration requirement is repeated in art.56 TFEU dealing with the right to provide services. This provision deals with a company established in one Member State providing service of an industrial, commercial or professional nature in another Member State. The main difference with services is that in contrast to establishment the company is entering another Member State only temporarily to pursue this activity.

Article 293 EC, now repealed by the Lisbon Treaty required the Member States to negotiate conventions with each other in order to secure uniformity of recognition of business practices across the Community (now Union). The article specifically mentioned the mutual recognition of companies within the meaning of art.48(2) EC. As a result of this requirement a Convention on the Mutual Recognition of Companies and Bodies Corporate was signed in 1968 by the six founder members of the European Community. However, it is not in force as it was not ratified by the Member State. Given this failure but recognising the importance of company law, the policy of the EU has been to move forward on the basis of directives dealing with specific matters. The fact that over 13 directives have been proposed reflects the extensive programme of harmonisation of company law embarked upon by the European Union. Although not all of these directives have been adopted, those which have cover such technical matters as company capital, company accounts, appointment of auditors and disclosure of information. These are important because companies established or providing services in different Member States facing the need to adjust to different regulatory regimes may lead to duplication of accounting, licensing and other requirements. This would act as a disincentive to penetrating other national markets. It may also reduce the opportunities for benefiting from economies of scale.

Another way of seeking to reduce the problems for companies operating in more than one Member State is to establish EU corporate structures. Regulation 2137/85 took the first step in this development with the establishment of European Economic Interest Groupings (EEIGs). These EEIGs permit companies and others to co-operate within the Community on a cross-border basis, and thus provide a vehicle for joint ventures. EEIGs have the mixed characteristics of companies and partnership. They are not separate in the sense that the companies are still liable for the debts of the EEIG but they do have a separate legal capacity. Such Groups have to be registered, which in the UK is a requirement to register with the Registrar of Companies. An EEIG cannot have more than 500 employees or offer any share participation to the public. Obviously there are certain limitations with EEIGs but they do provide a flexible vehicle for economic activity.

The ultimate aim of the EU is to have a new company formation which will have legal capacity throughout the Community. This is the European Company or Societas Europaea (SE), which is established by registration with the European Court in Luxembourg under a distinctive European Community company statute. Even though registration is with the Court, the SE could be domiciled in a particular Member State. The role of the SE is to facilitate cross-border co-operation by means of large-scale mergers and associations. It can be seen that this is perhaps the natural extension from the EEIG, which facilitates such ventures, but on a smaller scale. There have been some criticisms of the establishment of SEs, which led to delay in the adoption of the necessary Community legislation. However, the proposal was given a new impetus at the Nice IGC and in October 2001 the Council adopted the Regulation and Directive on the SE which came into force in October 2004.

REVISION CHECKLIST

You should now know and understand:

- [ ] **the right of establishment and freedom to provide services under arts 49–54** TFEU
- [ ] **the impact on individual professionals, companies and bodies corporate**
- [ ] **the importance of the principle of non-discrimination**
- [ ] **the right to receive services as interpreted by the CJEU**
- [ ] **the application of the rules to vocational training**
- [ ] **the impact of the** Mutual Recognition Directive
- [ ] **the right as applied to lawyers and companies**
- [ ] **the role and possibilities for the European Company or Societas Europaea**

SUMMARY OF KEY CASES

Case	Court	Key Principle
C-24/86 Blaizot v University of Liege	CJEU	Academic work at a university level can be vocational–for the national court to decide.
C-415/93 Bosman	CJEU	Rules which limit the number of professional players from other Member States are in breach of free movement of workers.
C-212/97 Centros Ltd	CJEU	Company formed in accordance with the legal requirements of one Member State has to be recognised as such by other governments.
C-118/75 Criminal Proceedings against Watson and Belman	CJEU	The action by the Member State must be proportional.
C-51/96 and C-191/97 Christelle Deliège V Ligue Francophone de Judo et Disciplines ASBL (the Deliège case	CJEU	It is not essential that the person who receives the services be the person who provides the remuneration.
C-29/83 Gravier v City of Liège	CJEU	Any form of education which prepares for a qualification for a particular profession, trade or employment...is vocational training.
C-286/82 and 26/83 Luisi v Ministero del Tesoro	CJEU	Private funded medical treatment is funded by art.56 TFEU.
C-76/90 Manfred Säger v Dennemeyer & Co. Ltd	CJEU	'Art.56 TFEU requires the elimination of all discrimination against a person on ground of his nationality..'
C-60/00 Mary Carpenter v SS for the Home Dept	CJEU	There was a cross-border element which was sufficient for MC to rely on EU law.

C-313/01 Morgenbesser [2004	CJEU	Under art.49 TFEU the Member State must undertake an examination of the qualification obtained ion the other Member State.
C-11/77 Patrick v Ministere des Affaires Culturelles	CJEU	There is an obligation on the Member State to compare the qualification gained in another Member State.
R. v Secretary of State for the Home Office, Ex p. Dannenberg	Court of Appeal	Recommendation for deportation quashed because failed to give reasons.
R. v Secretary of State for the Home Department, Ex p. Flynn	Court of Appeal	Any breach of the freedom to receive services would be a breach of arts 56 & 57 TFEU.
C-55/94 Reinhard Gebhard v Consiglio dell'Ordine degli Avvocati e Procuratori di Milano	CJEU	The rules relating to establishment are in line with those relating to services.
C-2/74 Reyners v Belgian State	CJEU	Art.49 TFEU is directly effective.
C-36/75 Rutili v Ministre de l'Interieur	CJEU	Free movement rights entailed a right of entry and residence in the whole territory of a Member State.
C-79/85 Segers	CJEU	Excluding a director of a company from a national sickness insurance benefit scheme solely on the ground that the company in question was formed in accordance with the law of another Member State are prohibited.
C-71/76 Thieffry v Conseil de l'Ordre des Avocats a' la Cour de Paris	CJEU	T had an equivalent qualification and training therefore absence of a French law degree could not exclude him from practice.

C-90/76 Van Ameyde v UCI	CJEU	The existence of national provisions which restrict participation of individuals of other Member States are incompatible with the provisions of the Treaty relating to competition, the right of establishment and the freedom to provide services.
C-36/74 Walrave and Koch v Association Union Cycliste Internationale	CJEU	The rule of non-discrimination on the grounds of nationality did not affect composition of sports teams.
C-372/04 Watts v Bedford Primary Care Trust (2003	CJEU	Medical treatment is a service and therefore subject to art.56 TFEU.

QUESTION AND ANSWER

QUESTION

How has EU law addressed the issue of the right of establishment?

ADVICE AND THE ANSWER

Introduction—The EU is founded on certain economic principles which promote economic activity by individuals and companies. The Treaty protects this right and is supplemented by various administrative measures as the Community attempt to deal with the problems experienced by professionals and companies in exercising their business activities.

Initially the EU attempted to harmonise rules associated with particular sectors but this proved to be very slow due to the difficulties of dealing with established professional groups and traditions.

The CJEU played its part in developing the case law associated with the right of establishment. For example where it held that a Dutch national resident in Belgium with the appropriate qualifications to practice law could not be debarred from his professional activity on the ground that, according to Belgian law, a lawyer must be a Belgian national (*Reyners v Belgian State*). Similarly the Court ruled in the case of a Belgian lawyer (*Thieffry v Conseil de l'Ordre des Avocats a la Cour de Paris*) and a British architect qualified to practise in France (*Patrick v Ministere des Affaires Culturelles*).

As with all freedoms granted under the Treaties there are circumstances where the Member State can seek the power of derogation. However, these must be proportionate and must not be used to provide a barrier to the right of establishment. The idea of mutual recognition of qualifications gained in one Member State to be recognised in another Member State has been applied to professional qualifications and to degrees (*Ministere Public v Auer*). It has also been used to ensure that companies lawfully registered in one Member State are recognised in another (*Centros Ltd* case).

EU law has addressed the issue of the right of establishment by building upon the base provided by the Treaties in arts.49–54 TFEU, introducing the specific legislation to deal with specific professions, such as the Lawyers' Establishment Directive 98/5, and the case law of the CJEU.

Sex Discrimination

11

INTRODUCTION

The EU Treaty has always been concerned with discrimination and the CJEU has said that one of the fundamental human rights is non-discrimination. The initial impact was on the area of sex discrimination and equal pay. The types of discrimination have been extended but sex discrimination remains the focal point of anti-discrimination legislation. This chapter reviews the law on sex discrimination.

The Treaty rule

In art.3 TEU reference is made to the underlying principles of the Union and the principle of equality. This indicates the special status given by Community law to the principle of equality. The specific article dealing with equality in employment is art.157 TFEU. Article 3(3) TEU states that the Union's aims include "It shall combat social exclusion and discrimination, and shall promote social justice and protection, equality between men and women, solidarity between the generations and protection of the rights of the child".

Pay is defined in art.157(2) TFEU as the ordinary basic or minimum wage or salary and any other consideration, whether in cash or in kind, which the worker receives, directly or indirectly, in respect of his employment from his employer.

The term "consideration" should not be interpreted too restrictively as it has been held by the CJEU to include other benefits such as favourable rates for family travel for railway employees (Case 12/81 *Garland v BREL*). As long as the "pay" has been (1) received by the employee in respect of his employment and (2) received from the employer, it will come within the meaning of the article. Thus it includes pensions paid under a contracted-out private occupational scheme (Case 262/88 *Barber v Guardian Royal Exchange Assurance Group*). (See also Case 7/93 *Beune*.)

In Case 43/75 *Defrenne v Sabena* the Court of European Justice held that the article has direct effect, the Court has identified a right which can be enforced by the individual employee in the courts of the Member State. Madame Defrenne had been employed by the Belgian airline Sabena as an air hostess. She complained of being paid a lower salary than her male colleagues although the work they did was the same. In an art.267 TFEU reference the Belgian court asked if art.157 TFEU could be relied upon before national courts. In its judgment the court said that discrimination on the grounds of sex could be indirect and disguised discrimination or direct and overt discrimination. The latter type of discrimination was more easily identified and could be based solely upon the criteria of equal work and equal pay referred to in art.157 TFEU. In such cases art.157 TFEU was directly effective and gave rise to individual rights which national courts must protect. It was necessary for additional measures to be taken with regard to indirect discrimination. This was achieved initially by the Equal Pay Directive 75/117 which supplements art.157 TFEU and this has now been replaced by Directive 2006/54 (see below).

KEY CASE

CASE 129/79 MACARTHYS LTD V WENDY SMITH

Facts: Smith was employed by Macarthy's wholesale dealers in pharmaceutical products. She claimed equal pay with the man who used to do her job and who she replaced as he received more pay for doing the same job. Smith was paid £50 per week whereas her male predecessor had received £60. The employer refused her request as under UK legislation the requirement was for the male and female workers to be doing the same job at the same time if a comparison was to be made. Smith brought a complaint before an industrial tribunal and then a subsequent appeal to the Court of Appeal where a request for a preliminary reference was made to the CJEU.

Held: the Court held that the only issue was whether or not the work was "equal" and it did not matter whether or not the man and woman whose work and pay were to be compared were employed at the same time in the undertaking or not.

Commentary: This case is another example where the CJEU required a national court to disapply national law in order to enforce the rights that had been given to the individual employee by EU law. The right to equal pay is provided by art.157 TFEU (then art.119 EC) and has direct effect.

In Case 127/92 *Enderby v Frenchay HA* the Court held that the burden of proof, which is normally on the claimant, might shift to the employer where that is necessary to avoid depriving workers who appear to be victims of discrimination of any effective means of enforcing the principle of equal pay.

KEY CASE

CASE 170/84 BILKA-KAUFHAUS GMBH V WEBER VON HARZ

Facts: Weber was a female part-time worker at a department store who was seeking to challenge her employer's occupational pension scheme. Although the scheme was non contributory for full-time employees with the employer paying all the contributions, this was not the case with part-timers. Under the scheme, only part-time employees who had been employed by the company for at least 15 out of a total of 20 years could qualify. She brought her claim to the German Labour Court arguing that pension scheme was contrary to art.119 EC (now art.157 TFEU) and the principle of equal pay.

Held: The Court held that the benefit constituted consideration paid by the employer to the employee in respect of her employment and thus came within art.119 EC (art.157 TFEU).

Commentary: In this case the Court provided guidelines to assist in identifying what might constitute objective justification for such differences in pay. The onus is on the employer to prove that the difference in treatment corresponded to a genuine need of the enterprise.

In Case 171/88 *Rinner-Kuhn* art.141 EC (ex 119 EC) was also held by the Court to be applicable to a statutory social security benefit. This case also included a part-time employee who was employed as a cleaner. She challenged the German legislation which permitted employers to exclude workers who worked less than ten hours per week from entitlement to sick pay. Despite statements in Case 192/85 *Newstead v Department of Transport* that social security schemes were outside the scope of art.157 TFEU, the Court held that sick pay fell within the article. Therefore the German legislation was contrary to art.157 TFEU. In an action brought by the Equal Opportunities Commission in 1994, the House of Lords held that the qualifying periods of employment in the UK's Employment Protection (Consolidation) Act 1978 were contrary to EU law. This was because they differentiated unfairly between part-time and full-time employees.

In *Barber* a group of male employees challenged their employer's contracted-out pension scheme. The employer's scheme was a substitute for the statutory scheme and was payable at different ages for men and women. The Court held that since the worker received these benefits from his employer as a result of his employment, the fact that the benefits were payable at different ages for men and women resulted in a difference in pay. Following this case it would appear that the only social security pension schemes provided for workers which fall outside the scope of art.157 TFEU are those which provide for workers in general, as a matter of social policy.

Following the *Barber* and *Bilka-Kaufhause* cases there have been a number of important developments. In Case 200/91 *Coloroll Pension Trustees Ltd v Russell* it was held that art.157 TFEU applied to occupational pension schemes and confirmed that survivors' and dependents' benefits constitute pay under the article. In Case 57/93 *Vroege v NCIV Institut voor Volkshuisvesting BV* and Case 128/93 *Fisscher v Stichting Bedrijfspensioenfonds voor de Detailhandel* the exclusion of married women and part-time workers from occupational schemes was also contrary to art.141 EC (now art.157 TFEU)).

However, in Case 249/96 *Grant v South-West Trains Ltd* the CJEU rejected the claim by a female employee with a female partner for rail benefits to which heterosexual couples were entitled. The Court stated that references to "sex discrimination" was not a reference to gender orientation. This was confirmed by Case 264/97 *D v Council* where the Court said that it was "unfit" as a judicial institution to bring about a positive change which was properly to be enacted by legislation. However, in *Chief Constable of West Yorkshire Police v A* [2004] UKHL 21 the Court of Appeal held that the Equal Treatment Directive covered discrimination against a transsexual. In Case 117/01 *KB v NHS Pensions Agency* the CJEU held that British legislation that prevented post operative transsexuals from marrying in their acquired gender could be a breach of EU "sex" discrimination law.

LEGISLATION HIGHLIGHTER

Directives

The basic role of the EU Treaty has been developed and refined by a number of directives. The Directives listed below illustrate how the EU has developed its policy by gradually widening the rights for EU citizens.

Directive 75/117 on equal pay for men and women has now been replaced by **Directive 2006/54** but was important in establishing a number of principles. Article 1 of this Directive provided for the elimination of all discrimination on the grounds of sex with regard to all aspects and conditions of remuneration. This Directive defined the scope of art.157 TFEU and introduced the principle of equal pay for work of equal value. Thus this directive met the points raised by the CJEU in *Defrenne* as to why art.157 TFEU could not apply to indirect discrimination. The UK government implemented this Directive by means of the **Sex Discrimination Act 1975** but not to the satisfaction of the Commission who brought proceedings under art.258 TFEU (see

Commission v UK). This resulted in the **Equal Pay (Amendment) Regulations 1983** which empowered a panel of independent experts to prepare a report on whether or not any work was of equal value to that of a man in the same employment (see Case 96/80 *Jenkins v Kingsgate).*

Directive 76/207 on equal treatment for men and women as regards access to employment, vocational training and promotion, and working conditions. The principle of "equal treatment" is defined as meaning "that there shall be no discrimination whatsoever on grounds of sex either directly or indirectly by reference in particular to material or family status". The important case of Case 152/84 *Marshall v Southampton and South West Hampshire AHA* was brought under this Directive. The Court in this case held that the Directive was directly effective as the employer was an emanation of the State (see Ch.4 above, p.43). In the subsequent Case 271/91 *Marshall v Southampton & South West Hampshire AHA No.2,* Mrs Marshall successfully challenged the UK legislation which limited the compensation paid to those individuals who had been discriminated against on the grounds of sex. This Directive has been amended by **Directive 2002/73** which attempts to bring EU sex discrimination law into line with the other forms of discrimination.

Directive 79/7 on equal treatment in occupational and social security schemes. This Directive applies to the working population both employed, and self-employed, and includes those whose work has been interrupted by illness, accident or involuntary unemployment (Case 208/90 *Emmott v Minister for Social Welfare).* There are exemptions to the principle of equal treatment, e.g. the determination of pensionable age for the granting of retirement pensions. This Directive has made little impact upon the various forms of indirect discrimination (see Joined Cases 63/91 and 64/91 *Jackson and Cresswell v Chief Adjudication Officer).*

Directive 86/378 on equal treatment in occupational social security schemes. As "occupational pensions" are to be considered as "pay" under the *Barber* judgment, the importance of this Directive has been reduced.

Directive 86/613 on equal treatment in self-employed occupations. This Directive extends the application of **Directive 76/207** to the self-employed.

Directive 92/85 provides a uniform level of social protection for pregnant workers and those who have recently given birth. Under art.10 of this Directive a pregnant worker, whether full-time or part-time, may not be dismissed. The new **Equal Treatment Directive 2002/**

73 has links with the less favourable treatment principle with regard to pregnancy. The Directive defines direct discrimination as where one person is treated less favourably on grounds of sex than another is, has been or would be treated in a comparable situation.

Directive 2006/54 is termed the **Recast Directive** because it recast the existing legislation on equal pay, equal treatment, and occupational social security and is principally concerned with providing remedies for those who feel that they have suffered discrimination. It codified the previous legislation and case law.

Application of the sex discrimination rules

In response to the *Barber* case and its implications for employers and pension funds, a Protocol was annexed to the TEU to limit its impact. It states that:

> "For the purpose of Article 157 TFEU ... benefits under occupational social security schemes shall not be considered as remunerations if and in so far as they are attributable to periods of employment prior to May 17, 1990, except in the case of workers or those claiming under them who have before that date initiated legal proceedings or introduced an equivalent claim under the applicable national law."

In addition the **Protocol on Social Policy** added by art.6 of the Agreement attached to it, purports to permit a Member State to maintain or adopt measures discriminating in favour of women in certain circumstances. The precise meaning of this is unclear, especially as the UK explicitly excludes itself from this Protocol. In Case 177/88 *Dekker* the CJEU held that refusal to employ a woman because she was pregnant was per se direct discrimination on grounds of sex under art.2(1) of the **Equal Treatment Directive**. As pregnancy was something which could only happen to a woman, refusal to employ because of Dekker's pregnancy was direct discrimination. Similarly in Case 179/88 *Handels-og Kontorfunktionaerernes Forbund v Dansk Arbejds-giverforening* (the *Hertz* case) the dismissal of a woman because of her pregnancy was ruled by the Court to be direct discrimination. If there had been another reason for the dismissal, such as absence from work through illness originating in pregnancy this would not be direct discrimination. In Case 32/93 *Webb v EMO Air Cargo (UK) Ltd* the CJEU reaffirmed that dismissal for reasons of pregnancy is illegal. Case 147/02 *Alabaster v Woolwich Plc* said that pay awards made while the woman was pregnant had to be taken into account when determining her pay.

REVISION CHECKLIST

You should now know and understand:

☐ **the principle of equality as found in the Treaties**

☐ **the impact of art.157** TFEU

☐ **the Directives that have developed the law of sex discrimination, especially the Equal Treatment Directive**

☐ **the application of the sex discrimination rules**

SUMMARY OF KEY CASES

Case	Court	Key Principle
C-147/02 Alabaster v Woolwich Plc	CJEU	Maternity pay must take into account any pay increases during maternity leave.
C-262/88 Barber v Guardian Royal Exchange Assurance Group	CJEU	Unlawful to have different retirement ages for men and women where occupational pension schemes are concerned.
C-7/93 Beune	CJEU	By the direct effect of art. [157 TFEU] there is equal treatment for the payment of benefits under a pension scheme.
C-170/84 Bilka-Kaufhaus GmbH v Weber von Harz	CJEU	The onus is on the employer to prove that the difference in treatment correspond to a genuine need of the enterprise.
Chief Constable of West Yorkshire Police v A [2004] UKHL 21	House of Lords (now the Supreme Court)	The House of Lords held that the Equal Treatment Directive covered discrimination against a transsexual.
C-264/97 D v Council	CJEU	
C-43/75 Defrenne v Sabena	CJEU	Art.157 TFEU held to have direct effect.
C-177/88 Dekker	CJEU	The refusal to employ a pregnant women is direct discrimination.

C-127/92 Enderby v Frenchay HA	CJEU	
C-208/90 Emmott v Minister for Social Welfare	CJEU	Until a Directive has been properly implemented the Member State cannot rely upon national time limits to deny a claimant.
C-128/93 Fisscher v Stichting Bedrijfspensioenfonds voor de Detailhandel	CJEU	The exclusion of married women and part-time workers from occupational schemes is contrary to art.157 TFEU.
C-12/81 Garland v BREL	CJEU	Pay should not be interpreted too restrictively—includes other benefits such as favourable rates for family travel for railway employees.
C-249/96 Grant v South-West Trains Ltd	CJEU	CJEU rejected the claim by a female employee with a female partner for rail benefits to which heterosexual couples were entitled.
C-179/88 Handels-og Kontorfunktionaerernes Forbund v Dansk Arbejds- giverforening (the Hertz case)	CJEU	Dismissal of a woman because of her pregnancy was ruled by the Court to be direct discrimination.
C-63/91 and 64/91 Jackson and Cresswell v Chief Adjudication Officer	CJEU	Benefits paid to boost earnings of low paid are not directly linked to unemployment.
C-96/80 Jenkins v Kingsgate (Clothing Productions) Ltd).	CJEU	Indirect discrimination justified to encourage full-time workers, greater mobility, training, etc.

C-129/79 Macarthys Ltd v Wendy Smith	CJEU	The national court to disapply national law in order to enforce the rights that had been given to the individual employee by EU law.
C-152/84 Marshall v Southampton and South West Hampshire AHA	CJEU	"equal treatment" is defined as meaning "that there shall be no discrimination whatsoever on grounds of sex either directly or indirectly by reference in particular to material or family status".
C-271/91 Marshall v Southampton & South West Hampshire AHA No.2	CJEU	Marshall successfully challenged the UK legislation which limited the compensation paid to those individuals who had been discriminated against on the grounds of sex.
C-192/85 Newstead v Department of Transport	CJEU	Social security schemes were outside the scope of art.157 TFEU.
C-171/88 Rinner-Kuhn	CJEU	Pay includes statutory sick pay
C-57/93 Vroege v NCIV Instituut voor Volkshuisvesting BV	CJEU	The exclusion of married women and part-time workers from occupational schemes is contrary to art.157 TFEU.
C-32/93 Webb v EMO Air Cargo (UK) Ltd	CJEU	Dismissal for reasons of pregnancy is illegal.

QUESTION AND ANSWER

QUESTION

Review the development of EU law on sex discrimination.

Introduction—one of the fundamental principles of the EU is that of equality. Since the Treaty of Rome in 1957 a key aspect of this has been art.157 TFEU which deals with equal pay. However, as the *Defrenne v Sabena* case demonstrated this article is limited in the way it can deal with indirect discrimination in modern society. This has led the EU to introduce a range of legislation to deal with these more subtle areas of discrimination on the grounds of sex.

The main example of the secondary legislation is the Directive 2006/54 on equal treatment for men and women as regards access to employment, vocational training and promotion, and working conditions. The principle of "equal treatment" is defined as meaning "that there shall be no discrimination whatsoever on grounds of sex either directly or indirectly by reference in particular to material or family status". The important case of Case 271/91 *Marshall v Southampton and South West Hampshire AHA* was brought under this Directive.

Other legislation has developed the principle of equal pay, such as Directive 75/117 (now Directive 2006/54) on equal pay for men and women. Article 1 of this Directive provides for the elimination of all discrimination on the grounds of sex with regard to all aspects and conditions of remuneration. This Directive defined the scope of art.157 TFEU and introduced the principle of equal pay for work of equal value. Thus this directive met the points raised by the CJEU in *Defrenne* as to why art.157 TFEU could not apply to indirect discrimination (*Jenkins v Kingsgate (Clothing Productions) Ltd*).

The latest piece of legislation is Directive 2006/54, which is termed the Recast Directive because it recast the existing legislation on equal pay, equal treatment, and occupational social security and is principally concerned with providing remedies for those who feel that they have suffered discrimination. As well as these examples there have also been legislation dealing with the rights of pregnant employees as demonstrated in the case of *Webb v EMO Air Cargo (UK) Ltd*.

The Maastricht Treaty on European Union and Beyond

12

INTRODUCTION

As the Treaties are the primary source of European law it is important to recognise the incremental changes that have taken place since the 1950s. This chapter provides a review of the most significant changes since the Treaty on European Union (TEU) and the attempts in recent years to provide a Constitutional Treaty.

The TEU was signed in Maastricht on February 7, 1992 and came into force on November 1, 1993. This was later than anticipated by art.52 TEU (ex R(2)) due to delays in ratification caused by referendum in Ireland, France and Denmark, and legal action in the UK and Germany. For the first time it became legally correct to refer to the European Community since this is the new name under art.8 TEU (ex G(1)) for the European Economic Community. The word economic was dropped to reflect the fact that there had been a change of emphasis towards non-economic provisions such as citizenship.

The TEU was the result of two regulation conferences, one on political union and the other relating to economic and monetary union. The TEU articles were numbered alphabetically to avoid confusion with the founding treaties which it amended. The result was that the treaties of the Community were lengthy documents and quite complex. The Treaty of Amsterdam had resolved this by completely renumbering the EC and EU treaties, which is why both the old and new article numbers are given in this book so as to avoid confusion.

Treaty of Amsterdam

The original TEU signed at Maastricht was reconsidered at an inter-governmental conference (IGC) in 1996/1997. At the IGC held in Amsterdam in 1997 the governments of the Member States negotiated about the changes to the TEU. The Treaty of Amsterdam came into effect on May 1, 1999. The main pressures on the negotiations were:

1. As indicated above, some Member States experienced problems in ratifying the Maastricht Treaty due to the feeling that the EU was not relevant or accountable to ordinary people. The Treaty of Amsterdam

attempted to deal with this by emphasising employment within the Union (see art.2 TEU and Title VIII EC). Reference was also made to sustainable development with regard to protecting the environment.

2. Applications had been received from ten former central and eastern European states plus Turkey and Cyprus for membership of the Union. This potential enlargement of the Union could not be accomplished within the then institutional structure.

The changes to the institutions are dealt with in Ch.2 above, p.2, but there are some others which were not to come into operation until there had been enlargement to 28 Member States. In relation to the European Parliament the number of MEPs had been fixed at 700 regardless of the number of states, although this was increased to 732 by the Treaty of Nice (now 751 under the Lisbon Treaty). Therefore, there was a need to be some reallocation of seats to accommodate new members of the Union. The European Commission was also to be affected by making it one Commissioner per Member State, thus removing the extra Commissioner enjoyed by the UK, Germany, France, Italy and Spain. As far as the Council of Ministers was concerned there was to be more emphasis on qualified majority voting (qmv).

Main points from the amended **TEU**

Acquis Communautaire art.2 TEU (ex art.B) explicitly refered to acquis communautaire, a principle which had been previously associated with the accession of new Member States. There is no formal definition of the term but it goes beyond the formal acceptance of Community law to include rules which have no binding force. These would include recommendations and opinions of the Council and Commission, resolutions of the Council and common agreements of the Member States. Some writers believe that the term has more of a political than a legal meaning. Perhaps the development of the Union into the fields of co-operation in foreign policy, Justice and Home Affairs measures has brought about the need to ensure that Member States work closely together. How it will work in practice will become clearer as the Community acts on these policies.

Subsidiarity

Article 5 EC (ex 3(b) EC) now states that:

> "... the Community shall take action, in accordance with the principle of subsidiarity, only if and in so far as the objectives of the proposed action cannot be sufficiently achieved by the Member States and can therefore by reason of the scale or

effects of the proposed action, be better achieved by the Community".

This article follows the statements in the Preamble that:

"... the process of creating an ever closer union among the peoples of Europe in which decisions are taken as closely as possible to the citizens in accordance with the principle of subsidiarity".

As it is the European Commission which makes proposals, it would appear that the onus is on it to justify its action at Union level rather than leaving it to the Member States. This could perhaps lend to a challenge in the European Court of Justice on the grounds that the proposed EU measure offends against the principle of subsidiarity. The Treaty of Amsterdam has a Protocol on the application of the Principles of Subsidiarity and Proportionality. This builds upon the guidelines developed in recent years and gives them the force of law. The Protocol cites three criteria for judging whether the conditions have been fulfilled:

1. Does the action have transnational aspects that cannot be satisfactorily regulated by the Member States?
2. Would action by the Member States or lack of action conflict with the requirements of the Treaty?
3. Would action at Union level produce clear benefits?

Amendments to the EC Treaty

1. Change in name. The term economic is dropped, as the Community is now to be known as the European Community (art.8 TEU). This change acknowledges the reality of today when Community competence is no longer restricted to the economic domain. The areas of activity in the amended art.5 EC (ex 3 EC) show extension to citizenship, social cohesion and social development, and the environment.
2. Article 1 TEU states that the Union is "founded on" the Communities, supplemented by the policies and forms of co-operation established by the TEU. Unlike the European Community under art.281 EC (ex 210 EC), the new Union does not have legal personality. Article 5 TEU (ex E TEU) makes it clear that the Union operates under or through the institutions of the Community. However, the objectives of the Union are wider than those of the EC, notably in the fields of foreign and security policy and justice and home affairs.
3. Article 6 (2) TEU (ex F(2) TEU) requires the Union to respect fundamental rights, both as guaranteed by the European Convention on

Human Rights and Fundamental Freedoms and as they result from the constitutional traditions common to the Member States. This article repeats much of the language used by the CJEU in its case law relating to the protection of fundamental rights as a general principle of Community law.

4. Article 7 TEU (ex F(1) TEU) requires the Union to respect the national identities of its Member States. This idea complements the principle of subsidiarity (art.5 EC) but also includes the cultural heritage of the Member States. It also recognises that the system of government found in all Member States is based on the principles of democracy.

5. The Treaty of Amsterdam includes a Protocol that encourages closer ties with the national parliaments of Member States. There is to be a six-week interval between the tabling of any legislative proposal and appearance on the Council agenda. This will give national parliaments an opportunity to hold a debate and thus contribute to wider discussion of legislative proposals.

6. The European Union is to conduct its activities on the basis of "an open market economy with free competition".

Citizenship of the Union

The TEU contained five new articles 17–21 EC (ex 8 to 8(d) EC), concerning citizenship of the Union. Although citizenship of the Union is established, the rights conferred and the duties imposed are those that flow from the EC Treaty. This is because the main impact is by the amendments the TEU makes to the EC Treaty and not as an independent Treaty. These do not materially affect the existing rights of economically active persons (see free movement of workers and the right of establishment above, pp.129–159).

Citizenship of the Union is mandatory for all nationals of the Member States; there is no provision for opting out. However, the Treaty of Amsterdam has amended the EC Treaty to reflect the point that citizenship of the European Union will complement and not replace national citizenship. All Union citizens residing in a Member State of which they are not a national have the right to vote and stand as candidates in both municipal elections and elections to the European Parliament in that State.

KEY CASE

CASE C-34/09 GERARDO RUIZ ZAMBRANO V OFFICE NATIONAL DE L'EMPLOI (ONEM)

Facts: Mr Zambrano and his wife are both Columbian nationals. In 1999 they entered Belgium along with their first child on a visitor's visa from Columbia. Shortly after the arrival of the family in Belgium Mr

Zambrano made an application for asylum. The application was refused, and an order issued requiring Mr Zambrano to leave the country but with an order that he was not to be repatriated to Columbia. Zambrano did not comply with the order issued against him and took up full-time employment in Belgium in 2001, despite having been refused a residency permit and consequently being ineligible to receive a work permit.

In 2003, whilst irregularly resident in Belgium, Mrs Zambrano gave birth to the couple's second child, followed by the birth of their third child in 2005. In accordance with Belgian national law both of these children acquired Belgian nationality at birth.

The dispute in the proceedings before the referring tribunal concerns a claim made by Mr Zambrano to receive unemployment benefit but the more important question was whether he had a right of residence in Belgium during the period of time over which he was in employment and had made the necessary social security contributions.

The main issue referred to the CJEU was whether Mr Zambrano derived a right of residency in Belgium under EU law following the birth of his EU citizen children in 2003 and 2005, notwithstanding that the children had yet to exercise their right of free movement within the Union.

Held: The CJEU based its judgment on art.20 **TFEU** and said that Zambrano has a right of residence in Belgium and the right to receive a work permit under EU law. Art.20 **TFEU** precludes any national measures which have the effect of depriving citizens of the Union the genuine enjoyment of their rights their status as EU citizens confers upon them.

Commentary: The concept of EU citizen rights has been developed in the Treaties but also by the interpretation given to those rights by the CJEU. In this case the Court seems to have significantly extended the scope of those rights because the parties involved are not exercising any rights of free movement or any cross border activity, but are involved in what could be seen as an 'internal matter' for Belgium. In this case a third country national who has children who are citizens of the EU through their birth has acquired the right to remain in Belgium and receive a work permit.

If the Union citizen is in a third country where the Member State of which he is a national is not represented, he is entitled to protection by the diplomatic authorities of any Member State, on the same conditions as that State's own nationals. (They can also access the European External Action Service

(EEAS).introduced in the Lisbon Treaty). There is also the right to petition the EP and to apply to the Ombudsman who was appointed by the Parliament in 1996 under arts 21 EC (ex 8(d) EC), 194 EC (ex 138(d)) and 195 EC (ex 138(e)). The Ombudsman has wide-ranging powers of inquiry and can request documents and evidence from Community institutions. He is empowered to act as a conciliator between citizens and the Community administration and can, if appropriate, refer a case to the EP. Every citizen of the Union has the right to write to the EU institutions, including the Ombudsman, in their own language and to receive a reply in their own language, which is assumed to be one of the 12 official languages. (There were23 official languages following recent enlargements but this has now been increased to 24 with the accession of Croatia in 2013.)

Three pillars

The TEU makes the point that the Union is built on three pillars, like a temple. The first pillar is the European Community as it now exists, the second refers to home affairs and justice, and the third to a common foreign and security policy. It should be noted that these two latter areas of policy are inter-governmental bodies and are not covered by the voting procedures in the Council of Ministers or as binding on Member States as other areas of EC Treaty policy. However, with the Treaty requirement for Member States to work together within a common position the decisions of these inter- gov-ernmental bodies are important. The European Commission is associated with the work of these bodies and the European Parliament is kept informed. The home affairs and justice policy includes policies on asylum, drugs, refugees and terrorism. It is claimed that with the completion of the internal market and the removal of border controls, there has to be common European Community approach to these problems. The co-operation on justice and home affairs introduced by the Maastricht Treaty was incorporated into the Union by the creation of an "area for freedom, security and justice" by the Treaty of Amsterdam. This was achieved over a period of five years, although under specific protocols the UK, Ireland and Demark were excluded from this development. The object was to make it easier for European citizens and nationals of non-member countries to move freely, while at the same time building up effective co-operation on border controls, asylum and immigra-tion matters and the fight against international crime. This has been achieved by the incorporation of the Schengen Convention 1990 into the EU Treaty. Thus only police and judicial co-operation will remain under the third pillar, but to which the Treaty of Amsterdam now adds "preventing and combating of racism and xenophobia".

A common foreign and security policy (CFSP) was in its infancy in the original TEU and the Commission and the Council wished to establish the machinery for "joint action". The reality of the post-Yugoslavia disintegration showed that this needed amendment, with the aim of providing an effective and coherent external policy. The Treaty of Amsterdam introduced more efficient decision-making based on qualified majority voting and the safeguard of "constructive abstention". This is designed to improve the ability of the EU to defend its interest on the international stage. The post of High Representative for the common foreign and security policy has been created to resolve some of the problems with the CFSP by providing continuity. Lastly, the common commercial policy was also extended to include services and intellectual property rights in the new art.133 EC. This will help in negotiations within the World Trade Organisation.

Treaty of Nice

The IGC at Nice in 2000 led to the Treaty of Nice being approved in February 2001. Although there were problems in ratification in Ireland these were resolved. The Irish government held a referendum in June 2001, as required by the Irish constitution, but this resulted in a "no" majority. However, in October 2002 another referendum provided a positive response to the Treaty of Nice. Therefore all Member States had ratified the Treaty by the end of October 2002.

The main emphasis of the Treaty of Nice was to prepare the way for the enlargement of the EU. In 2004 the number of Member States increased to 25 and in 2007 increased to 27. As the result of the political reluctance to grapple with the problem, the institutions had remained largely the same since the time when there were only six Member States, but the impending enlargement concentrated the minds of those heads of government meeting at Nice. The main implications for the EU institutions arising from the Treaty of Nice are:

1. The European Parliament—as a result of the decision to cap the number of MEPs to 732 on enlargement of the existing Member States, with the exception of Germany and Luxembourg, had the number of elected representatives reduced.

2. The Council of Ministers—from January 1 the system of decision by qualified majority voting was modified. This meant that in future a qualified majority would be secured when the number of votes in favour is close to the present threshold of 71 per cent and the majority of Member States vote in favour. In addition a Member State may ask for verification that the qualified majority comprises at least 62 per cent of the total population of the EU. If this is not the case the measure will not be adopted. The policy areas requiring qualified majority voting were also extended.

3. Co-decision procedure—in order for the EU to become more democratic

those policy areas that were now to be subject to qualified majority voting in the Council would also give more authority to the European Parliament by making them subject to the co-decision procedure.

4. The Commission—from 2005 onwards it was proposed that the Commission would consist of one Commissioner per Member State. 'When there are 27 Member States the number of Commissioners will not be one per State, but will be on a rotation system based on the principle of equality'. The EU was then 27 Member States and although this should have meant that there was some rotation at the appointment of the next Commission in 2014 there was some opposition to this, especially from the smaller Member States. The President of the Commission has also been given greater authority to organise the internal administration of the Commission and can request a Commissioner to resign if he has the support of the remainder of the Commissioners to do so.

5. The Court of Justice—with the increasing case load and resulting delays for cases to be heard the impending enlargement would only make this worse, even with the increased number of judges. Therefore, to ease the workload of the Court of Justice the Court of First Instance (now the General Court) was allowed to receive requests for preliminary rulings in certain specific areas. For the latter's workload to be reduced there was to be a number of specialist chambers or panels to take over the jurisdiction for staff cases and possibly some aspects of intellectual property. (See chapter 2 above).

6. Closer co-operation—some believed that this would lead to a two-speed Union but the Treaty of Amsterdam allowed for the possibility for a number of Member States to establish a closer co-operation between themselves but within the framework of the Treaty. The Treaty of Nice has extended this within the second pillar of common foreign and security policy. A minimum of eight Member States is needed to form a closer co-operation. The veto mechanism to stop this closer co-operation has been abolished as each Member State now has the right to refer the matter to the European Council. If the matter comes within the EC pillar of the EU the European Parliament must give its assent to the development.

Convention on the future of Europe

At Nice there was a "Declaration on the Future of the Union", which was followed up in December 2001 by the Laeken Declaration. The result was that the European Council decided to convene a Convention on the Future of Europe. The task of this Convention was to consider the key issues arising from the EU's future development and to try to identify the various possible responses. The membership of the Convention was drawn from the EU institutions and the national parliaments and governments. The Convention presented a draft Constitutional Treaty that was signed by the heads of government in October 2004 but it did not come into force because all Member States did not ratify it. Although some Member States did ratify the Treaty by Parliamentary procedure the referendums in France and the Netherlands in May 2005 rejected the Treaty. The Treaty has become academic even though it included some important developments in respect to the appointment of a full-time President of the Council and more involvement of national parliaments, which were seen by some commentators as ways of dealing with the "democratic deficit" suffered by the EU. An attempt to resurrect some parts of the Constitutional Treaty was made in the Reform Treaty, which was an amending treaty and did not replace the previous Treaties. This attempt has too foundered on a referendum held in June 2008 by the Irish government, as required by the Irish Constitution. Some attempts were made to put pressure on Ireland to hold another referendum to pass the Treaty, as it did in 2002 for the Nice Treaty. However, this was politically impossible until after the general election taking place then in Ireland and would be opposed by some even then.

The Lisbon Treaty

The Constitutional Treaty did not become law because it was never ratified by all the Member States. However, the necessary ratification by each Member State was scuppered when referenda in France and the Netherlands voted against it. A "period of reflection" was established so that each Member State could carry out a broad debate. The subsequent Treaty of Lisbon was not going to be subject to the need for referenda in Member States, with the exception of Ireland where such a popular vote is required under their constitution. In June 2008 the Irish Republic had voted against ratifying the Treaty of Lisbon. This was not the only Member State which had encountered delays in the ratification of the Treaty as Germany, the Czech Republic and Poland all had problems. Although Poland did ratify the Treaty if the goals of the Treaty of Lisbon were to be achieved ratification had to be accomplished in all then 27 Member States.

In December 2008 the concerns of the Irish people were set out by the Irish Prime Minister to the European Council which agreed that provided the Treaty of Lisbon did come into force these concerns would be met. Perhaps the most important concession to be incorporated into a legally binding protocol to be attached to the next accession treaty was that the Commission shall continue to include one national of each. On October 2, 2009 the Irish people voted by 67.1 per cent to 32.9 per cent in favour of ratifying the Treaty of Lisbon. The German Constitutional Court gave a ruling in June 2009 that the Treaty of Lisbon complied with the German Constitution but some aspects of the "accompanying laws" would require further national legislation. This was achieved by September 2009 allowing Germany to ratify the Treaty. At the European Council meeting at the end of October 2009 the concerns of the President of the Czech Republic were settled by agreement for action to be taken at the conclusion of the next Accession Treaty by way of protocols annexed to it. To satisfy the Czech President's concern these protocols will contain the statement that competences not conferred upon the Union in the Treaties remain with the Member States and also add the Czech Republic to Poland and the UK as countries exempt from the Charter of Fundamental Rights.

On December 1, 2009 the Treaty of Lisbon finally came into force and the challenge that the European Union had set itself in the Laeken Declaration had finally been achieved. The new posts of President of the Council and High Representative of the Union for Foreign Affairs and Security Policy were introduced by this Treaty. The new post of President of the Council is dealt with in art.15 TEU alongside a number of changes to the European Council. Mr Herman Van Rompuy was the first holder of this office and in 2014 he was succeeded by Donald Tusk, the former prime minister of Poland. The first High Representative of the Union for Foreign Affairs and Security Policy was Baroness Catherine Ashton who followed on from Javier Solana, who held the position of High Representative for the Common Foreign and Security Policy and Secretary-General of the Council of the European Union from 18 October 1999 until the new Commission took office in 2009. The new High Representative has a much wider and prestigious role as art.18 TEU indicates. She is also responsible for the development of the European External Action Service (EEAS). In 2014 Italy's Minister for Foreign Affairs and International Cooperation Federica Mogherini succeeded Baroness Ashton.

On July 1, 2013 Croatia became the 28th Member State of the European Union. This meant Croatian representatives being appointed to the Court of Justice, General Court and the Commission plus other EU institutions and agencies. Croatian became a new official language, bringing the total to 24 languages.

REVISION CHECKLIST

You should now know and understand:

- [ ] **the main changes brought about by the** Treaty of Lisbon **with the two elements of the TEU and the TFEU**
- [ ] **the issues developed by the** Treaty of Amsterdam **and why they were considered important**
- [ ] **the three pillars of the** Maastricht Treaty

☐ **the main points of the** Treaty of Nice
☐ **the background to the Convention on the future of Europe**
☐ **the problems with the proposed Constitutional Treaty resulting in it not being ratified**
☐ **the** Reform Treaty **and the difficulties it encountered**
☐ **aspects of the** Lisbon Treaty

SUMMARY OF KEY CASES

Case	Court	Key Principle
C-34/09 Gerardo Ruiz Zambrano v Office national de l'emploi (ONEM)	CJEU	Court significantly extended the scope of the rights of 'citizens' because the parties involved were not exercising any rights of free movement or any cross border activity.

13

The European Convention on Human Rights

....

INTRODUCTION

For many there is confusion when the term European law is used in so many different ways. Sometimes the law being described has nothing directly to do with the European Union. The main example of this is in relation to human rights. Although all the Member States are signatories of the European Convention on Human Rights this is a separate organisation based upon the Council of Europe. This chapter attempts to deal with this confusion by explaining the key elements of the European Convention.

There is always confusion about the relationship between the EU and the European Law dealing with human rights. The media often compound the problem by referring to the European Court without recording the fact that they are referring to the court adjudicating on this convention sitting in Strasbourg and not the European Court of Justice of the EU based in Luxembourg. This chapter is intended to clarify the distinction.

Following the atrocities of the Second World War, there was an impetus for an agreement directed at protecting the individual rights of people in Europe. The European Convention on Human Rights was drafted in 1949 and was influenced by the UN Declaration of Human Rights adopted in 1948. It has been extended by a number of protocols since then. All the Member States of the EU are parties to the Convention.

The UK was a signatory to the Convention in 1950 and it came into force in 1953. The Convention is binding in international law. However, some legal systems treat international law differently from national or domestic law, i.e. depending upon whether a Dualist or Monist approach is taken (see Ch.4, p.46). Thus the UK, as a dualist system, had to specifically legislate with the Human Rights Act 1998 to make the Convention available in UK courts.

Human rights machinery

The original human rights machinery consisted of the Commission of Human Rights, which received and examined complaints about the infringement of human rights, and the European Court of Human Rights, which adjudicated on cases which were referred to it by the Commission. There is also the

Committee of Ministers of the Council of Europe, which consists of the Foreign Ministers of the High Contracting Parties.

The increasing case-load prompted a reform of the Convention supervisory machinery. The outcome of the debate was the decision to abolish the Commission and create a single full-time Court. This Court is composed of 47 judges, which is equivalent to the number of Contracting States. The judges are elected by the Parliamentary Assembly of the Council of Europe for a term of six years, with half retiring every three years. The judges sit on the Court in their individual capacity and do not represent any State. Committees of three judges sit to carry out the filtering work formerly carried out by the Commission. The Court sits in chambers of seven judges, although in exceptional circumstances it may sit as a Grand Chamber consisting of 17. Where the Court finds that there has been a breach of the Convention, it has the power to order the offending State to make just compensation. If changes are necessary to domestic legislation, the offending state is free to determine what these should be in order to comply with its obligations under the Convention.

RIGHT OF INDIVIDUAL PETITION

Although initially the purpose of the Convention was directed at preventing large scale infringements of human rights by States which were party to it, the right of individual petition became effective on July 5, 1955. The UK recognised the right of individual petition in 1966. It is this right of individual petition that has given rise to the bulk of the cases coming before the Commission. This change of emphasis has led to the Convention being seen as a bulwark against specific infringements of human rights rather than large-scale violations.

Applications can be admitted from individual persons, non-governmental organisations or groups of individuals provided that the alleged violation concerns them directly. The application can only be brought against a Contracting Party to the Convention, i.e. a government or its agents. They cannot be brought against private individuals or bodies whose acts do not entail the responsibility of a Contracting Party.

As a "dualist" system the Convention did not become part of domestic law within the UK when the UK signed the Convention. However, as with other international treaty obligations, the Convention was applicable in the interpretation of statute law. This is based on the generally recognised principle of construction that Parliament does not intend to legislate contrary to the UK's international obligations. The House of Lords (now the Supreme Court)has indicated that where the law is either unclear or ambiguous, or concerns an issue not yet ruled on, the courts ought to consider the implications of the Convention (*Derbyshire CC v Times Newspapers Ltd* [1992] 3 W.L.R. 28). However, this situation has been superseded by the Human Rights Act 1998.

LEGISLATION HIGHLIGHTER

HUMAN RIGHTS ACT 1998
The aim of introducing the **Human Rights Act 1998** (HRA) was to make more directly accessible the rights which the British people already enjoy under the European Convention on Human Rights. The Act thus obviates the need to take human rights issues to Strasbourg.

Section 2 of the HRA requires courts and tribunals to take into account the "Strasbourg jurisprudence", i.e. previous decisions of the European Human Rights Court or the European Commission on Human Rights before its abolition. However, it is not just the courts and tribunals that are affected, as the Act requires a whole new culture to be developed by public authorities and government bodies. Section 3(1) states that "so far as it is possible to do so, primary legislation must be read and given effect in a way which is compatible with the Convention rights". It is no wonder that the implementation date for the Act was put back to allow public bodies, government departments and the courts to review their procedures and train their staff. It did not come into force until October 2, 2000.

Section 8(1) gives the courts wide powers, including the award of damages to injured parties:

"In relation to any act (or proposed act) of a public authority which the court finds is (or would be) unlawful, it may grant such relief or remedy, or make such order, within its powers as it considers just and appropriate".

The Convention and the EU

In 1976 the Commission ruled out the necessity of accession by the then Community to the Convention, but it did call for a joint declaration by the three political institutions affirming their commitment to fundamental rights. This Joint Declaration was made in 1977. However, in 1979 the Commission did formally propose accession to the Council and subsequently the European Parliament made statements supporting this development. However, the CJEU in its Opinion No.2/94 stated that as Community law stood the EU had no competence to accede to the Convention. In its Opinion the CJEU pointed out that although the original treaties made no specific mention of fundamental rights, the Court had in its judgments upheld the protection by way of general principles of EU law. Specific mention had also been made of the Convention in the Preamble to both the SEA and the TEU. This has been repeated in the Treaty of Amsterdam which amends art.6 TEU so as to reaffirm the principle of respect for human rights and fundamental freedoms. There is also the Charter of Fundamental Rights of the European Union, agreed at the Nice IGC. It reaffirms the commitment of the EU to the principles of the European Convention and other international obligations that affect the freedom of the individual. The unratified Constitutional Treaty 2004 included the Charter and so would have made it legally binding. However, the CJEU began to take the Charter into account in appropriate situations as illustrated by the case below.

KEY CASE

BOSPHORUS AIRLINES V IRELAND (2005)

Facts: A Turkish airline charter company, Bosphorus Hava Yollari Turizm (Bosphorus) leased and registered two aircraft belonging to a company residing in the Former Republic of Yugoslavia (FRY). One of the aircraft had been in Ireland for maintenance by a maintenance company owned by the Irish State, and it was seized under EC Council Regulation which had implemented the UN sanctions regime against the Federal Republic of Yugoslavia (Serbia and Montenegro). Bosphorus went before the Irish High Court claiming that the Minister's decision had infringed its right to respect for property. However, the High Court held that the EC Regulation did not even apply to the present case because the applicant's Turkish company was neither held nor controlled by a person or under taking from the FRY. On appeal by the Irish Minister of Transport, the Irish Supreme Court subsequently asked for a preliminary ruling from the CJEU.

Held: The ECHR held that the protection of fundamental rights by EU law was generally equivalent to that of the Convention system. Therefore there was a presumption that by enforcing the Regulation Ireland did not depart from the Convention as the Irish court was bound by the EU law. However, the ECHR left open the possibility that in circumstances where the Member State was exercising discretion when applying EU law they may be infringing the Convention. This would seem to put the onus on the Member State to consider its action in the light of the Convention when exercising any discretion it has under EU law.

Commentary: The ECHR seems to be drawing a distinction between the EU institutions acting in a particular way and those where the individual Member State decides to act on their own initiative or were exercising discretion. In this case they had no option but to enforce the Regulation as they were bound to enforce EU law. This case shows that the ECHR considered that the legal protection of fundamental rights had been established firmly within EU law.

The Treaty of Lisbon

Article 6 TEU specifically states that the EU will accede to the European Convention on Human Rights. The original European Convention was drafted on the basis that only individual states would accede, but Protocol 14 to the ECHR contains a provision which would allow an organisation like the EU to accede. The problems identified by the CJEU in its Opinion 2/94 were removed by the Treaty of Lisbon.

All 47 existing parties to the ECHR have to agree to the EU acceding and there is some concern amongst non-EU parties that the EU with its present 28 Member States would nominate the proceedings of the Convention. On the April 5, 2013 the final version of the Draft Agreement on Accession of the EU to the ECHR was presented to the negotiators representing the 47 member of the Council of Europe. There are some who argue that accession to the ECHR will strengthen the protection of fundamental rights within the EU; whereas others see it as something that is unnecessary and which will only extend the time needed for a judgment to be reached in some cases. The accession has to be agreed by all the members of the Council of Europe and the Council of the EU so the final date of accession is not yet known. On December 18, 2014 the CJEU delivered Opinion 2/13 on the draft agreement for the accession of the EU to the ECHR. Having noted that the Lisbon Treaty provided the legal basis for accession, the Court identified a number of problems which led it to conclude that accession by the EU to the ECHR was not compatible with EU law.

REVISION CHECKLIST

You should now know and understand:

- ☐ the background to the European Convention of Human Rights
- ☐ the human rights machinery
- ☐ the right of the individual to petition
- ☐ the Human Rights Act 1998
- ☐ the Charter of Fundamental Rights
- ☐ the relationship between EU law and the case law of the ECHR
- ☐ the relationship between the CJEU and the ECHR

SUMMARY OF KEY CASES

Case	Court	Key Principle
Opinion No.2/94	CJEU	CJEU argued that there was no power in the Treaties to allow for the accession of the EU to the ECHR—power now explicit in art.6 TEU.
Opinion No. 2/13	CJEU	Recognising that the Lisbon Treaty provided the legal basis for accession to the ECHR the CJEU said that there remained issues which meant that it was not compatible with EU law.
Bosphorus Airways v Ireland Application:45036/98	ECHR	The ECtHR held that the standard of protection of human rights within the EU was satisfactory.

Handy Hints and Useful Websites

14

When you have to answer a question on European law you should approach it on the same basis as any other legal question. In the introduction you should set the context of your answer by demonstrating that you understand the relevance or importance of the topic.

- For example if the question is on the "democratic deficit" of the EU you should explain what you understand the term to mean and the importance it has for the EU which is said to be based on democratic principles.
- You can then go on in the next paragraphs to review the main institutions of the EU and examine their democratic credentials. The European Parliament has been directly elected since 1979 but the Council of Ministers is not. The accountability of the Council is towards the national parliaments. Is this a form of indirect democratic control?
- The European Commission has been given a great deal of authority by the Treaties but it is appointed and not elected.
- The European Council is now recognised as a formal EU institution but these heads of government represent their Member States. They have been democratically elected but not for this role.
- In the final paragraph you can bring the main points of your answer together by looking at what has been done to deal with this deficit in the Lisbon Treaty such as giving more authority and influence to the European Parliament by the greater use of the ordinary legislative procedure which is an extension of the co-decision procedure introduced by the Maastricht Treaty and the European Parliament's involvement in the appointment of the Commission as discussed in chapter 2 above.

USEFUL WEBSITES

Some very good web sites for EU materials are:

The main site is http://europa.eu where you will find useful information on the history and enlargement of the EU but perhaps more importantly the Treaties and other documents like Regulations and Directives. It also provides links to the main institutions.

The European Court of Justice website http://curia.eu is where there is information about the cases reported in the Press Releases, law reports from the Court of Justice and the General Court, information about the personnel and jurisdictions of the courts. It is also possible to access the cases via http://www.bailii.org/ which is the web site for the British and Irish Legal Information Institute.

The European Commission website can be accessed via www.europa.eu or you can go direct via http://ec.europa.eu/index_en.htm. Here you will find information about the individual policies of the Commission as well as background information on the Commissioners and proposals for future policies. You might find it useful to look at the specific web sites for particular policy areas such as competition: http://ec.europa.eu/competition/index_en.html.

The European Parliament has a useful site which is getting better at providing information about debates and the involvement of the EP in passing legislation. It also provides details about the working of the EP and the individual MEPs: http://www.europarl.europa.eu.

The Council of the EU provides information about the Council of Ministers and the European Council—http://europa.eu/about-eu/institutions-bodies/council-eu/index_en.htm.

For a viewpoint from the British Government plus other resources the Britain in the European Union web pages of the Foreign and Commonwealth Office are generally good—http://www.fco.gov.uk/en/global-issues/european-union/.

A valuable resource is the website for the European Union Committees of the House of Lords. There are a number of Committees covering various areas of EU policy but a good general one is the European Union Committee on Law and Institutions—http://www.parliament.uk/parliamentary_committees/lords_s_comm_e.cfm.

Index

This index has been prepared using Sweet and Maxwell's Legal Taxonomy. Main index entries conform to keywords provided by the Legal Taxonomy except where references to specific documents or non-standard terms (denoted by quotation marks) have been included. These keywords provide a means of identifying similar concepts in other Sweet & Maxwell publications and online services to which keywords from the Legal Taxonomy have been applied. Readers may find some minor differences between terms used in the text and those which appear in the index.
Suggestions to **taxonomy@sweetandmaxwell.co.uk**.

189